The
Digital
Diet

The
Digital
Diet

The 4-Step Plan
to **Break Your Tech Addiction**
and **Regain Balance in Your Life**

Daniel Sieberg

Three Rivers Press
New York

Published in the United States by Three Rivers Press,
an imprint of the Crown Publishing Group, a division of
Random House, Inc., New York.

www.crownpublishing.com

THREE RIVERS PRESS and the Tugboat design are registered
trademarks of Random House, Inc.

Library of Congress Cataloging-in-Publication Data is
on file with the Library of Congress.

ISBN   978-0-307-88738-2
eISBN   978-0-307-88739-9

PRINTED IN THE UNITED STATES OF AMERICA

Book design by Ralph Fowler / rlfdesign
Cover design by Jim Massey

10 9 8 7 6 5 4 3 2 1

First Edition

For my darlings, Shanon and Kylie,

and everyone who helps

me untangle the wires

"For a list of all the ways technology has failed to improve the quality of life, please press 3."

—Alice Kahn, author of
Multiple Sarcasm

Contents

Contents

Step 4
Re: Vitalize

The
Digital
Diet

Step 1

Re: Think

You Are What You Type

*"Any smoothly functioning technology
will have the appearance of magic."*

—Arthur C. Clarke, author of
2001: A Space Odyssey

Brace yourself, for this is the wired world in which we live: for only $29.95 (plus shipping and handling) you can be the proud owner of the Wrist Cell Phone Carrier. What is the Wrist Cell Phone Carrier, you ask? I can best describe it thus: imagine gluing a wooden Popsicle stick to the back of your cell phone, so that the top half of the stick is attached to the phone and the bottom half of the stick is exposed. Like a cell-phone Pop-sicle. Then, while cradling the device in your hand as though you might make a call, use pink duct tape to strap the remaining stick portion to your wrist. There may be some Velcro involved, too, but that's pretty much it. This state-of-the-art accessory is designed to help you carry your cell phone everywhere you go and ease the strain on your arm and hand as you hold it next to your ear for prolonged periods.

Although this sounds like a story from the *Onion*, I assure you this is a very real product; I've seen it in the pages of a SkyMall catalog. It's for sale. People buy it.

Let's face it: the Wrist Cell Phone Carrier is indicative of our larger problem with technology dependence—we've become so attached to so many products and services that we need crutches to help us soldier on. It's all made us disconnected and disoriented. It's time to hit the reset button.

Plugged In, Checked Out

Before you stand on your soapbox (made of old video-game consoles or VCRs) and shake your fist in the air, please know that I'm not trying to stand in the way of the American dream of spontaneous consumption. I love technology and I always will. From Internet memes to video games. I've covered all things digital for more than a dozen years as a reporter for ABC News, CBS News, and CNN, to name a few, and I consider myself a proud geek at heart. But I've come to recognize that sometime in the last decade we've transitioned from being a culture that uses technology to being one that is completely absorbed by it. The sheer volume began to overwhelm us, and the swelling flood of gadgets and Web sites and doodads started to align into a force that invaded our lives.

The force hit, not like a nuclear explosion, but like the slow invasion of an ant colony. I've watched massive colonies of millions of army ants come to life at night in the jungles of Costa Rica. There is no noise, no perceived aggression, and not even a hostile undertone. They simply push forward and devour whatever is in their path. Now, is technology *killing* us like a wave of army ants? With a few exceptions, like distracted driving and mind-sucking YouTube videos, not literally. But it may be systematically, silently, and imperceptibly destroying parts of our lives that we hold dear.

It's time to look more deeply at our actions, to pull back for a time and then reshuffle our reliance on technology to make it work for us instead of the other way around. There's no turning back—the rate at which technology is infused into our lives will only accelerate. We need to accept that premise. Think of it like having to eat but empowering yourself to choose the best foods and mealtimes and following a steady exercise plan. The same goes for technology. The Digital Diet will help you turn yourself into a high-powered, high-efficiency communicator.

This book contains a plan for slimming down the use of everything from gadgets to social networks to video games in the hope of making yourself healthier, happier, and whole in the twenty-first century. To accomplish this goal, we will explore better tech management, examine ways to streamline use of everyday devices like your smart phone, and heighten awareness of how technology affects our (real) lives and those around us.

Through a step-by-step, dietary-style approach, the Digital Diet will help improve your connections with the world around you and the people you love. It's about being present in the moment—the moments that matter—and having the tools to maintain that mind-set for a lifetime. You'll learn how an overdose of devices and services has harmed our overall health: physically, mentally, and emotionally. To combat those effects, I'll introduce gadgets and applications that can enhance our lives. It's about embracing the stuff that works and shedding the stuff that doesn't. Think of it as "computing *POWER*," being aware of what all this technology is doing to you and your family and having the tools to make smart choices and manage your digital intake in the future.

Believe me, it's not too late to change course. And if you know the problem is larger than just you, then the Digital Diet can easily be expanded to include your children or your spouse or other family members, too. There is strength in numbers.

Will there be days when the Digital Diet falls apart? Of course. It happens to me and it will happen to you. There are days when I can't stand trying to limit my indulgence. And there are days when all my gadgets get the best of me. We're not cyborgs (yet). But just as you can eat that whole bag of sour cream–and–onion potato chips one night and opt for a chicken salad with pine nuts for lunch the next day, the same is true of the Digital Diet, since you can return to it after a lapse. It's a cumulative effect. A marathon, not a sprint.

Flashing Forward

It's possible that you're reading this book about re-fining your high-tech appetite through electronic means, like a Kindle or Nook or Sony eReader or iPad. You may have heard about it through a social network or a blog or an e-mail list. So you may be wondering if there's a contradiction in a message about streamlining technology "joining forces" with today's new media. Not as I see it. Remember that the Digital Diet is about moderation, not elimination; technology should liberate you, not inundate you. The purpose of this book is to reach as many people as possible and share ideas and revelations that I've gathered and refined. This guidance will naturally migrate online as you share your experiences and in turn help others and offer further suggestions and tips. A book about taming technology can therefore harness its breadth to spread a message (in other words, reading it on your Kindle or Nook is completely acceptable). In computer terminology, this book is not meant as a closed loop. I'm starting the chain reaction by writing, but the message should be shaped and molded and fine-tuned over time with the aid of the community at large, including online. Much like us, it's meant as a work in progress.

So why did you pick up this book? Was it the cover art? Was it the title? Was it on sale? Or was it because of an undeniable twinge saying your footing in technology feels increasingly like quicksand? I'm guessing the latter. You are not alone. In fact, you are well in the majority. You may also be worried about what an excessive dependence on technology is doing to your kids or siblings or friends. Maybe you're still not sure if you fall into this category. Let's see:

- Do you sometimes feel the urge to pull out your smart phone when someone else is making a point in conversation?

- Have you ever realized that you were texting while your child was telling you about her day at school and later couldn't remember any of the details of her story?

- Have you ever felt that something hasn't really happened until you post it on Facebook or tweet about it?

- Do you sometimes wonder if you could actually focus better in real life before all these gadgets invaded your space?

- Does a flashing red light on your BlackBerry make your heart flutter?

- Does a ringing/vibrating cell phone interrupt and trump everything else?

- Has looking left and right given way to looking up and down as you type on a smart phone and try to navigate a sidewalk?

- Do you often see the back of your child's (or spouse's) head silhouetted against the glow of a video game?

- Do you feel anxious if you're offline for any length of time?

- Do you know you shouldn't be texting and driving—but still do it?

- Do you find that your family can be in the same room but not talking to one another because you're each interacting with a different device?

If you (grudgingly) said yes to any of these questions, then you're among the millions of people who can relate to being overwhelmed by technology. Fear not—there is a way to shift your focus and find a better way of living with technology through a four-step program. It's time to make *peace* with technology, not war. Don't hate your phone or your e-mail or your Web services. Fold them into your routine and learn to tame them in a way that gives you authority. They serve *you*.

While we question what we eat or drink on a regular basis, we rarely question what this constant immersion in technology is doing to us. Think about it. Gadgets and Web sites don't come with nutritional labels. No one is regulating the amount of technology you ingest or how it's most effective for you. This book is meant as a guide to the technology in your life and aims to empower you to manage it and benefit from it. It's possible to trim your tech while still staying in touch, no treadmill required.

The tipping point for consuming technology has been reached, and our minds and bodies know when we've gone too far too fast. Think back to 1996, when cell phones and the Web were both delightfully extraordinary and totally foreign. We gleefully programmed voice mail and naively clicked on Internet ads. Something happened on the way to connectedness. No one said "stop." No one even said "slow down." Caught in the middle was the average consumer, who suddenly risked falling behind as the accelerating pace of technology took off like a viral video of laughing babies.

Flash forward to 2011, and I wonder how many of us still have cell phones from several years ago gathering dust. Recharger cables have become the scourge of the modern household. Too many to plug in, not enough outlets, and a damn mess when it comes to actually organizing them. We've struggled to create new passwords as old ones expire. We can't remember a day that didn't involve "www." I would love to extol the virtues of our wise and sage decisions when it comes to purchasing technology and finding a place for it in our lives and maximizing its uses. I really would. But I can't. Not on the whole. Don't take it personally—I'm lumping myself in there, too. We've blindly dashed through the gauntlet of gadgets and never once paused to catch our breath. Like a helpless lover who forgets everyone else around him, we've pursued our lust for all things digital.

How fast has it happened? In 2000, the percentage of people who had Internet access around the world was at about 48 percent. By 2010 it was up to 79 percent. In the United States, high-speed connections in the home hovered around 3 percent in 2000. Ten years later that figure had jumped to 63 percent. From 2006 to 2010 laptop ownership in the U.S. increased from 30 percent to 52 percent. Today, more than 85 percent of adults own a cell phone, 96 percent of eighteen- to twenty-nine-year-olds do, and more people are surfing the Web on the go versus sitting at a fixed computer. Lest you think these trends are all about younger people, the use of social networks by adults in the U.S. over the age of fifty jumped from 22 percent in April 2009 to 42 percent in May 2010. Clearly, in many ways we've become married to our technology. That doesn't mean a divorce is imminent—it means we need a prenuptial agreement.

Measuring Up

We each have different digital metabolisms. Disconnecting right away is like a starvation diet: lose the weight too fast and you gain it back. Therefore, when it comes to technology I loathe terms like "fasting" and "starving" and "off-lining." This diet is about achieving a balance. It's about maintaining a healthy consumption of technology. Yes, we'll discuss a "detox" period, but it's brief and meant to instill awareness.

The concept of limiting and trimming technology may sound hypocritical coming from a technology reporter whose job is to help people keep up with the latest and greatest, but that's the point—I've often been too eager to adopt every new gadget or trend simply because it's out there. Many of us fit somewhere in that spectrum. I don't think there is a perfect Digital Diet, but I've realized that we do need to regulate consumption. Cut here, add there. Too much of certain foods can be harmful. It's a no-brainer. So why not apply the same mentality to your binary calories? This book is about bringing more awareness, shining a light on behaviors and motivations, and searching for a "best practices" approach to our love of technology.

TechFact

The *New York Times* reports that the average computer user checks forty Web sites a day and switches programs up to thirty-six times an hour.

Technology isn't going away, and we're all in this together. This book is a manual, and I'm acting as your tech support (reporting for duty). You can extrapolate bits and pieces, decide not to do some of the exercises, or read it first and then go back and try the actual plan later. You also do not have to do it in exactly twenty-eight days. The time line is meant as a trail of bread crumbs—following these directives and exercises over roughly four weeks will lead you to a better place. But as with any dietary plan, you will only get out of it what you put in. At the core, the Digital Diet is about common sense and common courtesy. Impress yourself and those around you. Be the master, not the slave. Prepare to reboot and dig in.

My Binary Binge

"Ironically, with all this, 'We're now more connected than ever with technology,' I don't think we've ever been farther apart."

—Drew Barrymore

On July 4, 2009, my wife and I headed to a town called Boisson in the south of France to spend twelve days away from the distractions of New York City. We chose that rather remote spot because it's nestled in the rolling, sunflower-sprinkled hills of Provence (Van Gogh's backyard) and because her parents' friends owned a rustic cottage there and let us stay for free. Boisson is almost too quaint for words. Until you visit Provence it's hard to imagine that such towns exist—a charming church at the center, a nearby bakery, a handful of shops with cheese and baguettes, and narrow, winding roads that lead to tiny, ancient homes, each cuter than the next, with arched stone entries and wooden slats on windows. Boisson was meant to be the perfect place to disconnect from our modern world and focus on some old-fashioned reconnecting.

As the science and technology correspondent for CBS News, I was always on the go, always working on my next story for national television shows and running off to the next assignment. In hindsight, I realize that I stretched myself too thin and wasn't home nearly enough. I relied heavily on staying connected to my wife through my technology. It was about the occasional text message here or e-mail there. We were never big phone people and preferred to skip too much small talk. But after eight years together, the lack of more meaningful and special communication had become a problem in our marriage. We were distracted and dissatisfied. When we were apart, the way we used technology wasn't bringing us closer together.

Our trip to Boisson was designed to be a self-intervention, a crafted oasis from the ones and zeroes, and a time for my wife and me to rekindle our love and romance face to face. It didn't turn out that way. Next door to the town of Boisson was a campground that offered free, secured Wi-Fi to its visitors within range of the site's pool. Two days after our arrival I used my broken French to claim we were staying at the campsite and needed the Wi-Fi password. *Oui, s'il vous plaît?* It worked. And so for the remainder of our vacation I was often sneaking time online, lugging my laptop to the pool or using my iPhone. I felt bound by my work e-mail. Working in news means you feel a constant need to keep up with what's happening, and in technology that information moves pretty fast. I wasn't alone while I was online—my wife was nearby, often feeling neglected and shouting at me to join her in the water, threatening to submerse my gadgets. As the days went by, my wife's palpable frustration grew in direct proportion to my increasing Internet use. She made it clear that I seemed to be choosing the gadgets over her. This does not result in quality snuggle time.

Toward the end of our stay and during one of my devious Internet sessions, I received an e-mail from a producer at CBS News asking if I'd entertain the idea of swimming with sharks in the Bahamas for an *Early Show* series about conservation. I couldn't type "YES, ABSOLUTELY!" fast enough. I was especially excited because I'd taken the scuba pool and classroom training but hadn't completed the essential open-water dives. In other words, I'd been given the chance to finalize my diver training with tiger, lemon, and Caribbean reef sharks as my underwater cheerleaders. By contrast, my sunbathing wife groaned while simultaneously exhaling, "OH GOD." I couldn't tell if she was more annoyed that I was about to risk my life with sharks or that I was answering yet another work e-mail.

Two days later, our vacation over, we drove the five hours from Boisson to Nice in the wee hours of the morning to catch a plane to New York, where I dashed home to pack a bag (not forgetting my fins, wet suit, and mask), head to the Newark airport, fly to Fort Lauderdale, spend a few hours there, and then fly to Nassau. All told it took me thirty-two hours to travel from baguette-ville to Bahamian beaches. During that time I was back in full tech-guy mode, with gadgets in my pockets and a Bluetooth headset nestled in my ear, sending e-mails to friends and family (almost as last rites) and researching shark behavior (mainly the number of fatal attacks). After a snag with immigration in

Nassau, I eventually found myself on a small speed-boat en route to a spot known as Tiger Beach about twenty miles off the coast of West End, Grand Bahama. I had my BlackBerry in one hand, madly typing messages to everyone and posting status updates on my Facebook page, and was using the other hand to steady myself against the pounding waves. As we headed farther away from shore, I watched in abject horror—not as sharks surrounded the boat but as the bars of my cell-phone reception dropped from four to two to the dreaded "no service." I was cut off. It was the kind of disconnection that even rural Boisson hadn't provided.

Within an hour of getting to the forty-foot main boat, a crew member shouted, "Tiger! Tiger!" We looked over the side. Sure enough, the distinctive striped markings of a tiger shark could be seen through the shallow tropical water. And it wasn't just one shark—there were about a dozen lemon sharks, too, which are only slightly smaller and less aggressive. (With razor-sharp teeth, did it really matter which was which?) It was time to man up, suit up, and jump into the water without a cage to observe these marine predators up close. My diving "buddy" was experienced shark diver Stuart Cove, whose best advice was: (a) don't wave your hands around too much because they'll look like lunch, (b) stay right next to me, and (c) *BREATHE*. (The worst thing you can do as an amateur diver is hold your breath, since it can cause serious lung damage or worse.) Easier said than done when you're surrounded by some of the world's most efficient and effective predators.

While having a tiger shark swim within a few feet of you during your first open-water dive seems a long way from disconnecting from technology, I'm here to tell you there's a direct link. I had to focus on my breathing, my vision, and my movement. The pure basics of survival. It's a rare occasion in today's always-on world that we aren't allowed to let our minds wander or communicate with someone or pick up a smart phone. I know I hadn't experienced that sensation of being so cut off (aka focused) in many years. My life was a continual loop: seeking feedback, data, and interaction.

The tiger shark broke through that blabbering "bleep bleep bleep" clutter, and I'll never forget staring into its unblinking eyes. I had been told sharks are capable of sensing a racing heartbeat through the pulses it makes in the water. Exude calm, everyone had said. Yeah, right. All I wanted to do at that moment was Google whether hitting a shark on the snout really makes an ounce of difference if it attacks. For a split second I actually had the urge to use my BlackBerry underwater while a fearsome predator stared me down. (What the hell was wrong with me?) And then the thought was gone. I was lost in something I couldn't appreciate until my first dive: the silence. Just the sound of bubbles escaping here and there. Heartbeats. Breathing. Gurgling water. More breathing. Remember the breathing. Between being in near-paralytic awe of my imposing companions and steadying myself on the sea floor, I began to enjoy the connection with *me*. A pure thought process. The sheer survival. Face to snout. It's common knowledge that sharks have some of the sharpest teeth in the animal kingdom, but this one didn't even have to use them to cut my electrical cords. During the five dives we took with the sharks, my confidence actually went up. I had achieved a clarity of focus that may have helped me survive without losing a limb.

When I got back on the boat, we were still out of cell-phone range, so I was alone with my thoughts of adventure and excitement and mind-boggling "Did I just do that??" sentiments. That shark—that perfectly evolved, majestic tiger shark—was a call to action. I needed to be silent, to focus on connecting with *me*, without any digital interference. If I did, I'd feel stronger and more in control, as I'd felt during the dives. Then I wanted to call my wife and tell her how I'd graduated beyond the France intervention. I wanted to share my epiphany.

Despite my revelation, it wasn't until nearly six months later that I did anything about it. The experience had been shocking, but it hadn't been personal.

Happy Hollow-days

In the winter of 2009 it finally hit me—I was completely out of touch with what really mattered, full stop: the people I knew and loved. Despite the life-altering encounter with the sharks, I hadn't been able to hang on to that momentum when I returned to the real world. Over the next few months, largely thanks to my reimmersion in technology and work, I had lost track of my father getting remarried, a good friend's pregnancy, and my stepbrother's impending divorce. On the relationship side, my mild case of social anxiety, coupled with easy access to social networks, meant that I had lumped my full-time friends and family in with my casual friends and "fans" and treated them the same way.

By gathering them together at a site like Facebook (1,664 of them), I had flattened the definition of friendship and diluted their significance. My wife was somewhere between concerned and infuriated by my chronic preoccupied behavior—none of which was helpful as we were trying to start a family.

I kept trying to recall the way I had felt with the sharks, but it wasn't enough. Outwardly, I was the guy who connected with everybody; inside, I knew I'd actually lost connection with the people I cared most about. And I'd lost connection with my*self*. I couldn't take it anymore. Technology was becoming toxic. My primary poisons were social networks. I needed out.

How did I get there? Starting in early 2007, I'd say I was a heavy Facebook user, a regular Twitter user with just 866 "followers," and a rare MySpace user. Combined I spent anywhere from twelve to fifteen hours a week perusing these sites, reading updates, and sculpting my own Internet Adonis image. That's 725-plus hours a year, or close to thirty days. *THIRTY SOLID DAYS*. And what had I gotten out of all that surfing around? Apparently not as much as I thought. During the holidays in 2009 I met face to face with friends and family in Canada for the first time in many months. As we began to share our lives via the spoken word and not the keyboard, I realized how little I really knew about them.

The great irony is that many of them had Facebook profiles and some even read my Twitter feed and vice versa. *I thought we were connected.* But I rarely sent direct e-mails, which had become the new equivalent of getting a handwritten letter. Telling someone what I was up to or about our lives had become a chore, so I had resorted to simple status updates or tweets or, at best, mass e-mails. The epiphany for me was that I'd become a terrific broadcaster and a terrible communicator. In our 140-character Twitterverse the intimate details of their lives had escaped me. And isn't that the important stuff? Definitely more important than our geographical location or which restaurant we'd eaten at or, in my case, when I was appearing on a certain news program. There was an awful lot of telling going on and not a lot of listening.

But my ego and I had gotten sucked in. Big time. I'd allowed the passive acceptance of strangers to replace meaningful interaction with the people I knew and cared about. I had become more interested in a wall post here or a poke there. I'd also become a "friend voyeur." On Facebook I'd pore through people's photos and read about what they were doing and sometimes get jealous. I was torturing myself and trying to compete by constructing my superficial self. That's because social networks are like Pleasantville. Smiling faces, wonderful experiences, and happy happy happy all the time. Sure, there are the occasional posts that admit, "I'm feeling blue today," but by and large it's like a sprawling "digi-topia." And who wouldn't want to live there? My social networks had become a confusing blend of personal and professional. I didn't know who I was anymore. So shortly after the New Year in 2010, I left. I deactivated my profiles. The breakup was like "It's not you, Facebook, it's me."

The reaction to my announcement to quit was swift and intense—I heard everything from "Your career will fall apart" to "Why the CBS sci-tech guy?" to "I give it a week." Some were supportive. Some probably laughed. Some thought it was a midcareer crisis. But the weirdest thing was that so many people reacted as though I was, well, *dying*. "We'll miss you!" "What will we do without you?" "Don't go!" Their outcries did make me feel a little sad, until I thought about the fact that I wasn't actually going anywhere. The only thing that died that day was a bunch of ones and zeroes. I was still on TV and still writing online and still on the radio. The only

TechFact

In August 2010 comScore reported that Internet users spent more time on Facebook than on Google. A total of 41.1 million minutes, or 9.9 percent, of online users' time was spent on Facebook, compared to Google with 39.9 million minutes, or 9.6 percent, of users' time. This figure includes all Google properties, such as YouTube and Gmail.

difference was that I wouldn't be broadcasting my every move to 1,664 friends, most of whom I didn't even know.

On social-network sites you don't expose that you had a fight with your wife or that you're having job anxieties or that you're stressed out from financial pressures. But these sites can lull you into feeling like you've fulfilled your actual relationships or self-reflection with a quick sentence or two. They make us think that we know people or that they know something about us. It took swimming with sharks and tension in my relationship with my wife to make me realize that by relying on technology to communicate I was not being the son or the brother or the friend or even the husband that I thought I was.

My separation from social networks is what led me to research and pursue a greater understanding of the Digital Diet approach to technology. I know how this Digital Diet can help others because I've lived through it. Survived it is more like it. I've tried to come out the other side a stronger and better person. Still an avid fan and user of technology, but a better manager of my time and a better friend, on- and offline.

Your Raison d'Être

The Digital Diet is designed to guide you to a new life in four weeks. By mixing and matching pieces of the plan, you can customize it based on age, gender, profession, family size, demographic, hobbies, and income. Think of a recipe/diet book that outlines an overall food plan—it gives you options. The same goes here. Don't feel as though you need to adhere to every tenet, fulfill every exercise, or try every product. But I will offer all of them to you and encourage you to try as many as possible. And be honest with yourself. Force yourself to take on the challenges you know you need. The ripple effects could improve everything from your familial relations to your marriage to your work performance. The ultimate goal is to improve your*self.*

But before we explore the actual plan, it's time to take stock of how much time and energy and relations we've lost in our race to embrace technology.

3

The Weight
You Can't See

*"With iPods and iPads; Xboxes and PlayStations—
none of which I know how to work—information
becomes a distraction, a diversion, a form of
entertainment, rather than a tool of empowerment,
rather than the means of emancipation. All of this is
not only putting new pressures on you. It is putting new
pressures on our country and on our democracy."*

—President Barack Obama, May 2010

In recent years there's been a raging debate in
the tech world between those who believe we
need to unplug on a regular basis and those who say
plugging in is both necessary and advantageous. But

the argument between the two misses the point: the goal is moderation. I'm not advocating going "off the grid" or even eliminating technology for a while and then giving yourself permission to indulge later. My intention is to recognize the strengths and weaknesses of the online and offline worlds and teach you to recognize when operating in one rather than the other is a suitable option. Perfection isn't possible. But seeking betterment is.

Some experts argue that the way we live in the twenty-first century is no different from the way we lived a hundred years ago because it's relative. Back then we had to struggle with milking machines *and* a washboard. Or getting the mail *and* wanting to read a book. The difference is that those activities had a finite experiential window. People would stress about these pursuits or needs before they finished them, but once the physical act was complete—the book closed, the washboard down, the mail opened—it was on to another activity. Not so today.

Today we are part of the matrix. I don't mean the movie; I mean the endless web of questions about the kids' babysitter and birthday reminders and wondering if that accounting report is finished. We don't "tear ourselves away from work" anymore; our work tears us away from everything else. And there is often little sense of completion with work or other activities. We can adjust the time and place of a meeting instantly through text or e-mail, or we can change our mind about the color of a rug and order a new one. We can be reached at all times in nearly all places. Our connectedness often translates into a constant state of flux, and the decisions in our lives are rarely final. The technology that helps us stay in touch also makes us crazy by constantly demanding our time and attention. Just as we set up a Skype call so the grandparents can see the new baby, the boss e-mails and asks for an "emergency" update on the budget numbers. But there are ways to cut through the sticky strands and turn that web into an empowering weapon rather than a net (think Spider-Man).

Head in the "Clouds"

Information today is increasingly stored through "cloud computing." An obvious example is Web-based e-mail. Your Gmail or Yahoo! account is maintained by the respective company at remote locations/ servers. Your e-mail messages aren't actually stored on your desktop or laptop. Your e-mail provider

stores them and you can access them from anywhere. This is a popular model for everything from
word-processing documents to shared calendars to
PowerPoint presentations. Even digital music. The
idea is not only that the information isn't taking
up space on your computer but also that it can be
viewed and tweaked from anywhere, and by other
people around the world, too. Useful, certainly.

But the slippery slope is that we've always got our
head in the clouds. Recall for a minute that early period in the midnineties when checking your e-mail
meant physically going to your computer, logging
in, composing and sending the messages, and then
logging out. No one had a smart phone or a tablet.
Wi-Fi was extremely rare. We actually had to stop
talking on the phone while we dialed in to the Internet. It was all about getting in and getting out. A
clear demarcation. We've lost that line. All tasks, all
mediums, blend together.

Frustrating as that cloud may be, we must accept that it won't be clearing away. But what if the
forecast called for "scattered clouds" rather than
being "socked in"? You can learn to allow some sun
into your life by separating from the cloud once in a
while and connecting when necessary.

I have a problem with advice that calls for simply

turning everything off for a day (or a week). For some experts, that's the whole strategy. But when you power your gadgets and machines back on, the e-mails and texts and Facebook posts will still be there (*feed me, feed me*). It would likely be even more jarring to have to sort through your backlogged digital deluge without having a plan going forward. That's where this book plays a role: giving you that plan. Bottom line: stop the clouds from turning into a fog.

Family Tip

"Chill out"—the next time your son or daughter comes to the dinner table with a smart phone or iPod or laptop, try putting it in the fridge during the entire meal. It won't do any harm to the device. Then serve it as the final course, after the dessert.

E-obesity

It's not a revelation to say that this country has an obesity problem. But there is mounting concern that gluttony for technology is creating what I call the "e-obesity" problem. By that I mean that our increasing appetite for gadgets and the Web has made us lazy and less active. Most days, the only parts of our bodies that are getting a great workout are our fingers and thumbs, and they are often being overworked.

First let's look at the numbers as they apply to the young generation. The Pew Research Center's Internet and American Life Project recently found that half of American teenagers send more than fifty text messages a day and that one-third send more than one hundred a day. Every day. Add that up over a month and we're talking easily in the thousands. Two-thirds of the texters surveyed said they were more likely to use their cell phones to text friends than to call them. Fifty-four percent said they texted their friends once a day, but only 33 percent said they talked to their friends face to face on a daily basis (a probable harbinger of the death of "small talk"). The Kaiser Family Foundation reported that young people between the ages of eight and eighteen spend on average seven and a half hours a day using some sort of electronic device, from smart phones to digital music players to computers. In essence, they're online for the time spent at a full-time job, which is a number that likely startled many of you, even those who keep your smart phone in plain sight during waking hours.

The role of technology in childhood and adult obesity has now been proven without a doubt. More than forty studies have been conducted on the matter, and many indicate that the availability of technology contributes to a sedentary lifestyle and weight gain in children. A Canadian study conducted in 2003 and published in the *International Journal of Obesity* linked seven- to eleven-year-olds' television and computer use to a significantly increased risk of being overweight or obese. The study found that children who spent three or more hours a day using technology had a 17 percent to 44 percent higher risk of being overweight and a 10 percent to 61 percent higher risk of obesity.

It's not just about weight or teenagers. Accord-

TechFact

According to a report by the Consumer Electronics Association (CEA), the average U.S. household spent $1,380 on consumer electronics in the course of twelve months (between mid-2009 and mid-2010), which represents an increase of $151, or 12 percent, from the previous year.

ing to the U.S. Department of Labor's Occupational Safety and Health Administration (OSHA), repetitive strain injuries (RSIs) are the nation's most common and costly occupational health problem, affecting hundreds of thousands of American workers and costing more than $20 billion a year in workers' compensation. The UK's Chartered Society of Physiotherapy is so concerned about the phenomenon that it published a guide for phone users warning of "text message injury." Or how about cellphone elbow? From the same orthopedic specialists who brought you carpal tunnel syndrome, we now have cubital tunnel syndrome. The ulnar nerve runs under the funny bone to the fingers. When this nerve gets stretched by cell phone users holding a phone up to their ear for long periods, it can become weakened. Blood supply to the nerve can also be affected. The result is pain.

Need other examples of potential physical harm?

- Used at high volumes over an extended period, digital music players can damage hearing. (On occasion they have even interfered with pacemakers.)

- Big-screen TVs can be dangerous falling objects and have caused injuries to children.

- There is concern that the heat some laptops generate on the lap can cause fertility problems in men.

- Some laser printers emit particles from the toner that can damage your lungs. There are also ozone emissions from laser printers.

- Headaches, lower-back pain, and upper-body tension are all associated with spending long hours in front of a computer.

On the psychological and emotional side, many technologies and Web sites thrive because of our increasing interest in promoting ego and minimizing the importance of one-on-one contact. They offer themselves as a way to stay in touch with others and tell people what we're doing and generally bring people "closer" to you. But are they really?

Picture this scenario: You get a text message that reads: "I'm so sad that Gary and I broke up." [Beat.] Text: "I'm crying so hard right now that I'm shaking." [Beat.] Text: "I might just finish this bottle of pinot." [Beat.] Text: "My life sucks." This type of scenario happens frequently. But if your next instinct wasn't to pick up the phone or arrange to meet in person, then the experience of seeing your friend crying and in pain remains mere words on a screen. There's no way that's as powerful as seeing tears stream down her face into her wine glass and offering a consoling hug. The latter is tangible, visceral, and messy. And these days it seems we're too afraid to deal with that side of life. Technology makes life more sterile and makes it too easy to avoid a conversation (services like slydial send you straight to voice mail), face responsibility (sorry, didn't get your message), or display emotions (those emoticons just don't cut it). Too often technology allows us to replace meaningful interactions with superficial ones. Many of us have become terrible and ineffective communicators and bloated and selfish broadcasters. Lots of telling but

TechFact

"As far as I'm aware, there is no evidence that any kind of radio frequency radiation (including cell-phone towers, cell phones themselves, and Wi-Fi) cause any negative health effects," said Michael First, a professor of clinical psychiatry at Columbia University and editor of the *DSM-IV*, the diagnostic bible for psychiatrists.

very little listening. We've come to rely on what I call, in fast-food terms, "drive-through connections." Pull up, get what you want, and drive away. No fuss, no muss. If only real life were so convenient.

Charging Ahead

I encounter too many people who feel helpless in the face of change. They have this look like technology got the best of them and their family and there's nothing to be done about it. Anything they try feels like building a sand-castle wall to stop the incoming tide. That makes me angry. We're better than that. It's about surfing the wave, not running from it. There *is* a way you can fold in the wonderful aspects of technology while filtering out the harmful ones. It's about creating more awareness and building better structure. Getting there, though, starts with arguably the hardest part: when we (temporarily) tear things down with the detox.

Step 2

Re: Boot

4

Detox (Don't Be Afraid)

Days 1–2

"There is time enough for everything in the course of the day, if you do but one thing at once, but there is not time enough in the year, if you will do two things at a time."

—**Lord Chesterfield, 1740s**

This is the beginning of a journey aimed at asserting your control over technology, improving your communications, and taking back your real life. The dividends could last a lifetime.

The first step in the process involves powering

down. That's good news, I promise. During the next stage in the diet you will assign a value to each device and online tool. Those values will become part of your Virtual Weight Index, or VWI. Following that, the key part of the diet looks at which technologies are effective for you and your family, which ones are unnecessary, and which ones can be eliminated. Eventually I will outline a digital intake plan that you can tailor to your particular situation, lifestyle, and needs. That plan will very much let you stay in touch. Along the way, we will delve into brain and body exercises to relieve stress, and I'll offer plenty of fun tips and tricks to stay positive. In the end, you'll regain a balance to your life that has probably slipped away in the past decade.

The critical stage of the Digital Diet is the beginning, because it homes in on why you're here, assesses your current situation, and forces you to ask what you're afraid of giving up if you trim your tech (and even eliminate it for a short while). In the detox stage, the goals are: (1) highlight the amount of technology in your life, (2) appreciate what it's doing to your communication, multitasking, and self-worth, (3) imagine your life without technology by eliminating it from your life for a short period of time,

(4) briefly discover alternatives, and (5) establish boundaries with friends and family.

Onward.

Take Action: It's time to detox. First, put your personal devices and temptations in a box. That's right, a literal box. It can be a shoebox, or, if you're a bit more gadget heavy, then you can always use the top drawer of a dresser. And I mean everything—the cell phone, the BlackBerry, the laptop, the portable video game. Go on, I can wait. If you can't move something, like your video-game console or your desktop computer, then shut it down and put a garbage bag or something similar over it.

Now have a look at them. How do they make you feel? Likely a mix of emotions. Which are taking up the most of your time and energy? You may see some devices as both utopian and dystopian. Your smart phone is where you receive a photo of your niece playing soccer but also a reprimanding note from your colleague. For now, physically and mentally separate your*self* from your gadgets. Leave them in the box as we head to the next phase.

Take Action: It's time to invest in some low-tech tools—buy a durable (paper) notebook. Once you've powered it on (aka opened it), it will become your new laptop and a personal journal for the next couple of days, which is essential for releasing any pent-up frustration. Give yourself permission to explore the analog side of your life for a while. For ten minutes before you doze off at night or ten minutes in the morning, let it flow out of you, unfiltered and unfettered. Get in touch with whatever is coming to you without the digital stimuli around you.

Ask Yourself:

How are your face-to-face relations with loved ones?

How would you describe your reliance on technology?

Do you list "multitasking" on your résumé but loathe the very thought of it?

Are you worried about losing touch by going on the Digital Diet?

Jot down the answers to at least one of those questions at the end of your first night on the diet. At the end of each week I'll ask you to revisit them and gauge how the diet is affecting your life.

Wire Spaghetti

As you question how all these devices piled up and wonder what happened to your attention span, consider this: In 1998, the number of consumer-electronics products in the average U.S. home was six. By 2009, it was twenty-five. Sound too high? Glance over at that box and flip open that notebook. I want you to list all your household electronics (including the ones you've put aside). I'll start with my list, and then it'll be your turn:

1. coffeemaker

2. DVD player

3. HDTV

4. Xbox 360

5. portable iPod dock/radio

6. DVR

7. Apple TV

8. mini stereo

9. older cell phone

10. MacBook

11. Dell laptop

12. wireless router

13. iPod

14. digital camera

15. iPhone 4

16. iPhone 3GS

17. iPad

18. e-book reader

19. clock radio

20. GPS watch

21. desktop computer

It's not quite twenty-five, but it's pretty close. What's the tally for your family? Take a few minutes and write down your devices (include your children's) that require a charger or AC power. More than you thought? It's an overflow we all face. Those devices want our time and our concentration. Each of them represents a portal to a person or a source of distraction. If we're honest with ourselves, it's often hard to imagine living for very long without many of them. We need them for our family, our social life, and our job. It's a kind of symbiotic relationship, but just who is feeding whom? Some may have to go by the end of this diet. But we don't need to live without all of them. Nor can we. We just need to look at them differently.

As you review your list, it's also important to make a distinction between two types of technologies: those used for communication and those used primarily for passive entertainment or cooking. All of them are technically digital, but consider how often you turn off the coffeemaker versus turning off your smart phone. The latter demands your attention at random times, the former only when you're in the room. No doubt the communication ones may be harder to live without (although instant coffee qualifies as legalized torture in some countries), but think about how each of them makes you feel. And consider whether they're enhancing your life (and the lives of various members of your family) the way you'd like them to. The communication devices go in the box, but it's important to list the passive electronics as well and to think about them. They also take up your brain energy, though not as much.

TechFact

About 60 percent of kids between the ages of ten and fourteen have a cell phone, according to the Center on Media and Child Health. The next age group's usage is even higher, with 84 percent of those ages fifteen to eighteen having a phone.

Take Action: Now it's time for your passwords. I know this is another big step. Ordinarily I'd never advocate sharing a password (absolutely not for your banking or credit cards). But choose a trustworthy person in your life and let them temporarily change your social network passwords to remove any temptation. Think of it as a little break from the pressure of keeping up with the virtual Joneses. Not forever, although you may choose to even deactivate your profile for a while, as I did, just long enough to better understand its place in your life. Fear not—your avatar will still be there even when you're not logged in. Companies like Facebook and MySpace and LinkedIn have no vested interest in removing you and your wealth of personal data.

What About TV?

I should point out that TV and radio are okay during the detox. Obviously it's best not to become a total couch potato, but letting your mind get lost in a rerun of *Seinfeld* or catching the latest episode of *Glee* is fine. When I was growing up, my parents

Exercise Day 1

Before checking out, at the very beginning of day one, give yourself a chance to tune in. Find your favorite playlist on your player of choice and spend at least thirty minutes just listening to some music. Don't respond to e-mail and listen to music, don't "friend" people on Facebook and listen to music, and definitely don't text and listen to music. Take the opportunity to let the music wash over you, hear the lyrics, feel the beat. Use it to get motivated and fired up. Use it to chill out and let your mind wander. And you can return to that music anytime during the diet—it's about connecting within you rather than looking without.

probably wished there were a "TV diet." Certainly over the years there has been much debate about whether that passive zoning out is at all beneficial (for relaxation, not education). Generally when we watch, we're comfortably on a couch or cuddling with a loved one. It takes us away from the *bleep-bleep-bloop-bloop* and lets us unwind. That's not to say it's a great alternative to going for a walk or exercising or flying a kite. But it has a different place in our lives beyond our gadgetry and Web sites. Yes, there are Web services tied to TVs, but no cheating. Keep it to the broadcast and cable stuff.

Reach Out and Be in Touch

Perhaps most important during this stage, please be sensible about how and when you officially get under way. For example, you wouldn't go on a liquid diet right before a family reunion picnic. So don't attempt this project at the start of a busy workweek. Often a weekend works best, since the detox is only a couple of days. And please don't undertake this Digital Diet in isolation. In fact, do quite the opposite. Inform as many friends and family members as you can about your decision to make this change. Set up an out-of-office message saying you won't be online for the next couple of days (let them assume it's a vacation, if you'd like). And record an explanatory voice mail. Sure, some folks might initially snicker if you tell them what you're doing, but I can almost guarantee that at some point they will (a) be curious about how it works, (b) admit to their own feelings of overindulgence, and (c) ask how they can do it.

Since you've taken the time to stash your gadgets away and see them all together, you're now allowed to take your cell phone out of the box. You can use it during the detox phase, but only for calls and voice mail. Turn off the data plan. No sending texts. As for e-mail—checking once in the evening is okay, but that's it during the detox period. Resist. Focus on being in receiver mode only.

Excuse You

What I believe might surprise you about the next couple of days is how well the rest of the world copes without your being plugged in every second. People will go about their business, your family won't fall apart, and you can determine the weather by looking out your window instead of looking at

Re: Boot

a smart-phone icon. This is important in terms of establishing boundaries. You'll be surprised at how much stronger you start to feel, not bending to the whim of everyone else. Let them adjust. They'll survive.

Conversely, how you cope with the detox in a physical way might be a bit more difficult. There are studies that show people who disconnect experience feelings of disorientation, headaches, and anxiety. You're removing a regular stimulus to the brain, and it might be physiologically noticeable. This is perfectly normal. And it's not meant as punishment. Remember that the point is to instill a new awareness of your technology and how it permeates your life. Pick up a novel instead of your laptop. Lie down for a quick nap. Get some exercise. Engage in conversation that involves looking in someone's eyes. No one is suggesting this last for any more than a couple of days, but I assure you that those two days will prove insightful as you rethink technology's role in your life and better assess why it's there without any wires getting in the way.

Take Action: To help with those feelings, turn to your journal again and take note of what's motivating you to seek out technology. Are you feeling lonely? Are you unwilling to deal with your own thoughts and worries? Is it boredom? Force yourself to look inward when the going gets tough. And think about how your dependence on technology structures your day (e.g., what you would do first upon waking).

The natural world has much to offer, too. Going outside or doing a little people watching can be a

Exercise Day 2

Read the newspaper. (It's that folded object that gets ink all over your fingers.) Pull out the sections, sit in bed, and share it with a friend. Hell, read the whole thing. Remember to read the writer bylines and the location from which they filed the story. In an age when everything just "appears" online, it's easy to forget that people still have to provide that content, and some of them go to great lengths and distances to report it. Rediscover that there's something delightfully intangible about the tangibility of an actual newspaper. By the time our kids grow up, it may not be around in the same format.

great way to let your mind wander. I know it sounds corny, but even looking up at the clouds or the trees can open your mind and shake away the nattering echoes of your wired world. Take deep breaths and don't panic. Do your best to enjoy this time.

Something from Nothing

Now that you've simplified your tech environment and pushed aside those devices for a bit, let's examine an area of increasing study: multitasking. Are we better or worse off as a result of multiple technology inputs into our lives? Do we actually get more done?

Those who say we're often better off, like Jonah Lehrer, tech writer and author of *How We Decide*, claim that stimulating our brains in different ways can make us more creative and open to new ideas. Lehrer says we should sometimes put down our shields when it comes to resisting more high-tech influences in our lives, so that we'll be able to explore their effect on us in a practical way, see where it leads. And I believe that can be true—it's a bit like freestyle jazz, where our minds check out a travel Web site and then our bank account and then send a text and then read a friend's Twitter feed. Certainly it opens up many avenues of discovery.

On the other hand, some experts say all the digital multitasking hinders our ability to complete each independent task successfully. A study from Université Pierre et Marie Curie in Paris, France, published in the journal *Science* in April 2010 found that the part of the brain known as the medial prefrontal cortex essentially divides in two when faced with more than one task. But throw in more than two tasks and the brain gets a bit baffled. The phrase "jack of all trades and master of none" comes to mind. It's not that multitasking is entirely bad (and often it's quite necessary), but splitting your brain power can be taxing. Be aware of when it's too much, when your mind is beginning to feel overwhelmed. When that happens, take a break. Close every window except one.

The main problem with massive multitaskers, according to a Stanford University study from 2009, is that they're terrible at filtering out the stuff that doesn't matter. The study's authors found this group easily distracted and incapable of ignoring irrelevant information. (This likely comes as no surprise to anyone with a teenaged son or daughter.) The researchers first ranked people's multitasking intensity by asking how many types of media they used simultaneously (print, TV, computer, phone, text, etc.). On the low end were people who reported using in the neighborhood of 1.5 types of media at the same time. Serious multitaskers were juggling more like four. Sound familiar? For the test, they presented people with a series of red and blue rectangles, blanked them out, then showed them again and asked if the red ones had changed position. The high multitaskers couldn't ignore the distraction of the blue rectangles and often failed to get it right.

The researchers found that people caught up in multitasking constantly crave information but don't do well at processing it all. They referred to two distinct ways of receiving information: exploring and exploiting. Explorers (multitaskers) get a thrill from more and more data, while exploiters would rather ponder the information at hand. What about simply being faster at switching to a different task? Well, the researchers also asked the participants to classify a letter as a vowel or consonant or a number as even or odd. Indeed, even while trying to switch between questions the high multitaskers were slower. Much slower. No doubt to their amazement.

Their conclusion? For most of us, the more gadgets, the more distractions, the less effective we are. Does this mean we have to go through life in a purely linear fashion, fully completing every single task before taking on the next one? Of course not. Some multitasking is unavoidable. (As the father of an infant I know all about trying to accomplish as much as I can in a short amount of time.) But are other people questioning your productivity even as you feel busier than ever? The point is to keep tasks manageable and to a minimum. Rank their priority. Be efficient in following each task through to completion, rather than piling on more. Know your limits and recognize when multitasking is becoming detrimental. For example, send that e-mail to a colleague first, then check any incoming text messages. Take that phone call and then update your calendar. If you're old enough, think of Luke Skywalker on board the *Millennium Falcon* as he tried to deflect pulses sent from a flying robot using his lightsaber. After Obi-Wan Kenobi encouraged him to don a visor to block out distractions (Han Solo's chiding), he became a better Jedi. When possible, try to zap the tasks away one at a time (and then head into hyperspace).

With constant multitasking we have also become our own worst enemy. A 2004 study by the School of Information and Computer Science at the University of California at Irvine found that people are just as likely to interrupt themselves as to be interrupted by external forces. And with the rise of social media that likelihood has no doubt gone up. We're like gnats buzzing around and checking out the next online stimulus. Did someone just text me? Who wants to talk to me on instant message? Has someone I know updated their status? How many frequent flier miles do I have again? That same study found that on average in a typical day we spend only about three minutes on any given electronic task or pursuit. Informal interactions in person average just four and a half minutes each. Ever wonder where your day went? The answer is that it was spent in a lot of different places, never for too long. And the official name of that study? "Constant, Constant, Multi-tasking Craziness," which is the way one of the participants described his life to the researchers.

You need to become more aware of your multitasking limits—honestly assess whether you're really accomplishing a task or just fumbling through it. Sometimes, it's better to put it off and complete it later, at a more optimal time or on a more optimal device. Rediscover the power of singular focus and minimize the multitasking for a while. It comes as no surprise that studies show 95 percent of people

TechFact

A Harris Interactive study found that 72 percent of people identified bad mobile-phone behavior as one of their top ten pet peeves, but only 18 percent of mobile-phone owners admit they are guilty of displaying such behavior.

multitask at some time or another. But what started as a term for computer performance ("This machine can multitask those abstract financial calculations") shifted to being a matter of personal pride ("I'm an awesome multitasker") and has now morphed into a term filled with dread and derision ("I can't keep up with all this multitasking"). Wait, weren't our personal digital assistants supposed to make life easier and more manageable? It hasn't quite turned out that way. We've become like sound engineers, constantly adjusting the various dials and knobs that represent our lines of communication. But the volume has overwhelmed us.

The ultimate goal for the next couple of days, and indeed the entire Digital Diet, is to stare that shark in the eyes with clarity of focus. Strip away the distractions for a time and concentrate on whatever task you put your mind to. Spend time reading with the kids. Organize your closet. Pull out that musical instrument that's been gathering dust. Over the course of the coming weeks, your mission is to incorporate that mind-set into your technology, too, as it gets reintroduced and we explore new options for managing it.

To summarize this portion of the Digital Diet, surviving the detox is meant to be an accomplishment, and congratulations are in order if you can brave these two days and actually get something out of them. Some aspects will be positive and some will be negative. Some will remain questionable. But it's not the end. It's barely the beginning.

Carry on with forward progress.

5

Your Virtual Weight Index

Days 3–5

"Do you realize if it weren't for Edison we'd be watching TV by candlelight?"

—**Al Boliska, radio personality**

Richard Restak is a noted Washington, D.C., neurologist who has extensively studied the effects of technology on the brain. A part-time magician, Restak likes to ask people a series of questions to get them to think about their reliance on technology: When are you using it? How does it make you feel? Why do you need it? His point is to make people recognize the effects technology has on a deeper level, well beyond just the surface practicality of its function. It's cyber sleight of hand.

The Web means we're never really alone, and, Restak points out, that affects our self-confidence and our inner strength. With just a click, we can get stimulation from the online world, as well as instant gratification. For example, we've become less reliant on our ability to find out from other people which train to take because we can simply punch in some coordinates and be done with it. Everyone can agree that a Web site offering routes for public transit is useful and beneficial. But is this type of tech shortcut eroding our ability to ask questions and be curious about our surroundings? To think for ourselves and be resolute in our decisions? Our heads down, all too often we give in to our gadgets and let them be our guide.

But when we use our mind and our social graces to overcome a particular dilemma, like catching the right train, there is a sense of pride that *we* accomplished something, not our device. That's one key to better management of your digital life. Recognize those occasions when your brain is able to solve the problem, and rely on it. Don't automati-

Exercise Day 3

Do not use Google Maps or GPS or MapQuest for the next few days. Remind yourself of the power of the human compass and the exploratory nature of finding your way. Talk to people, ask for their help, and see where it leads. Write down directions before you leave the house. See what's around you. Just because seemingly every square inch of the planet has been digitally mapped doesn't mean you should stop interacting with the physical environment.

cally look something up. We're often tempted to take the path of least resistance when the greater reward will come with some effort—and lasting benefits. You won't lose yourself if you get a little lost.

"The brain is changing," Restak says. "It's not changing through genetics—it's too slow a time. We're not fruit flies; we don't multiply in a couple of weeks. So therefore, inheritance and genetics and biology are playing less of a role than technology. Technology is driving and forming—sculpting, as I like to call it—the brain." With that premise from Restak, we must take one step further and accept that we are creatures of change increasingly driven by external forces. This is particularly true of young people, whose brains are developing while they are surrounded by the lure of technology every day. Accepting this doesn't mean accepting that we've lost control. Therein lies the secret to the Digital Diet—*you* are in control. Listen to your inner voice, your mind, your body—all telling you that you've lost your balance. Watch your children and their behavior and don't be afraid to intervene. The cliché "everything in moderation" is a cliché because, like many others, it's true. Your brain will still feel the incremental effects of technology over time, but becoming more aware of them will at least provide you with a chance to recognize when they're harmful.

Response Time

Back in 1996 I can remember leaving the room while a photo downloaded via my 1,200-baud modem. It'd still be chugging away when I returned. I had patience; we all did. Waiting for a handwritten letter was like waiting for a little gold nugget to arrive in your mailbox. The time someone took to craft it, fold the paper, and choose a stamp helped the delivery feel personal and special.

That's all changed. Today we wake up in a sea of data. It surrounds us and binds and connects us. It calls to us like a cyber siren. But it can also swamp us and disorient us and drown us. Today, Restak says, we often get a hit of dopamine in our brain when people reach out to us through digital means. We begin to desire these messages and notes and postings above anything else and consequently ignore everything else around us. It can be all-consuming. Sometimes, says Restak, our brain just needs a break. A time-out, if you will.

Take Action: Inhale deeply and exhale slowly. Take another breath. And then one more. That probably took all of about twenty seconds, right? When was the last time you paused long enough to inhale some precious air, let it rest momentarily in your lungs, and then exhale it with the full force of your body? If you're like most people, it's probably been a while. Those deep breaths will likely be rather important as we plunge in with some tough and personal questions.

Your Computer Screen as Mirror

Let's examine how we view our real selves versus our online selves. I'm referring to the fine-tuning we do to portray our lives to those who "know" us on social networks—in essence, creating our avatars. Do you feel that your online postings truly reflect how you feel and think every day? How many times are you projecting "happy thoughts" to keep up appearances or make others jealous? When was the last time you experienced something and chose to reflect on it rather than post it on a social network?

So how about those 140 characters? When Twitter hit the scene in a big way in 2009, it asked users a simple question: "What's happening?" There were the early adopters who enjoyed telling people they were ironing their socks or rearranging their paper-clip collection. And we made fun of them. We yelled a collective "Who cares??" Then more and more people (myself included) got enamored with the idea of having "followers" and telling those followers exactly what we thought about some product or where we were going or how we were so incredibly bummed out that McDonald's stopped selling the McRib sandwich (again).

But suddenly we, myself included, started defining ourselves by the *number* of followers we had and clamoring for more. Gaining a follower became a challenge. What will this person think of me? Who are they exactly? Did it matter? A number is a number. And I got sucked in to the trap of wanting my number to go up and up and not really considering whether any real connection was being made. The more people who heard me, the more excited I got. Except that I wasn't actually hearing anything back. Sure, I clicked on links and made occasional comments on people's posts. But it quickly turned into a competition—who could tweet the wittiest comment about Tiger Woods's scandal? Who would be first to tell their followers that Michael Jackson was dead? Who was having the *MOST AWESOME FABULOUS FUN TIME AT SOME EXOTIC LOCATION??? ME, THAT'S WHO!!!* And by God, I was going to tweet about it.

At some point I got carried away with sites like Twitter and more concerned about how followers viewed my feed (my pseudopersonal story) than about what my actual life was like. The two began to blur together. I kept imagining my followers (866 of them) reading about me and therefore wanted to put my best binary face forward. I felt the need to be funny but still professional. But that's not real. What was anyone really learning about me? Nothing. And I certainly wasn't learning anything about them.

If you have a Twitter account, then I bet you know exactly how many followers you have, within a small margin. What do you really know about any of them? I don't mean to make it sound like we shouldn't share our lives with people we care about or vice versa. But let's remember that online personalities are not real. Period. And how about Facebook? It's become a place where we share everything about our lives. Perhaps we need to rethink what kind of information we share and how and when we share it. Worrying too much about our appearance or time on social networks is a mental weight that we don't need.

Your E-days

For the next twenty-eight days, I want you to think about the time you spend using technology as your e-day. During detox, your e-day is zero. As you build, day by day, toward a healthy digital balance in your life, your e-day will expand. Think about when it starts and ends now. Does your e-day start the moment you wake up, when your smart phone alarm goes off and you roll over and check your e-mail? Can you make it start later in the day, after breakfast, so that you have time in your life without digital input? By the end of this diet, you'll have a clear idea of how long you want your e-day to be and how to make sure your e-day is not your entire day.

Take Action: For the next two days, reintroduce the device or service you use the most for up to thirty minutes per day (outside of any critical work-related activities and time spent at the office). In addition, you can spend up to fifteen minutes per day on your other devices and services, for a total of a forty-five-minute e-day. Time yourself using your watch or an old-fashioned egg timer.

While you're enjoying your e-day, hold back from the mindless texts and needless status updates. Begin your postdetox phase with an awareness that you hope to sustain over the long run. Obviously you'll be surfing the Web during that time, but keep social networks to a minimum. (More on that shortly, as we delve into their effects on us.) Try to focus on your mind, your personal relations, and your own sense of being. Spend your forty-five minutes, get work or play done, then focus on the people and things in your immediate vicinity, and see how that makes you feel. During this stage we will also examine which specific technologies are over-whelming your life or your family's and try to come up with a workable formula for better management of them. But give yourself this chance to get off the ground with a solid start and a clean slate.

Take Action: Use this opportunity to do something you've wanted to do for a long time, like going for a hike, having a cozy dinner, taking a trip to a museum or show, or even building something. The catch is that you need to do it without then posting about it online. No sharing photos and refreshing Facebook to see how many people commented. Let the experience wash over you and process it inter-nally. Of course, you don't have to do it alone—call

TechFact

The average person today consumes almost three times as much information as the typical person consumed in 1960, according to research at the University of California at San Diego.

a friend or a family member. Just be social within your immediate surroundings. Does this change the value of the experience? Is it more or less meaningful as a result? Are you more or less confident? Keep asking yourself those tough questions. And don't be afraid of the answers.

Your Virtual Weight Index, or VWI

Currently, the most common and controversial measurement to determine obesity is called the "body mass index," or BMI. But what about all those gadgets and Web sites and services? Collectively a bunch of electronics might only weigh several pounds in your hand. But forget about gravity for a minute. Think of how they weigh on your *mind*. This is the basis for your VWI: your Virtual Weight Index. The following formula will help you tailor this Digital Diet to your situation. It's the key to personalizing everything going forward. Depending on your VWI, you might place more or less emphasis on certain exercises. And you might decide to skip certain ones altogether. The choice is yours. For now, let's examine the formula.

For every . . .

++ smart phone you own, add 3 points

++ social network you use, add 4 points

++ laptop you own, add 1 point

++ tablet or iPad-like device you own, add
2 points

++ e-mail account you use, add 2 points

++ cell-phone texting service you use, add
5 points

++ online role-playing game log-in you use,
add 7 points

++ desktop computer you own, add 1 point

++ e-book reader you have, add 1 point

++ digital camera you have, add 1 point

++ additional gadget you own that requires
a charger but doesn't fall into any of these
categories, add 1 point

++ blog you write or comment on, add
2 points

A personal VWI might look something like this:

iPhone 4 +3 points

LinkedIn, Facebook +8

Dell laptop +1

Gmail, Yahoo!, and work e-mail accounts +6

texting on iPhone 4 and work BlackBerry +10

Kindle +1

Canon camera +1

VWI = 30

That's a pretty typical profile of someone who needs technology as part of their job (a growing number of us) and enjoys keeping in touch on a regular basis. A low VWI at this stage would be <25 (your Digital Diet will streamline your usage and eliminate some stress), midrange 25–35 (your Digital Diet will help you stay sane and organized), and high 36 and up (your Digital Diet could be totally life-altering). Don't panic if you have a high VWI. Through the Digital Diet you may lower it dramatically. Or you may only drop a couple of points. The purpose is to add awareness to your routine and see the benefits. In truth, the VWI is probably more akin to your credit score than to your body mass index. You can make changes in your spending habits and minimize your reliance on borrowing money and see that number go up. But you might also want to close some credit cards or accounts if you don't use them. The one major variable in the VWI is your ability to monitor how often you use these gadgets and services. It's one thing to own them or sign up, but you don't have to rely on them. Remember, you are in control.

Take Action: Look at your VWI and circle the accounts and services you haven't used in six months. When you next go online, try to shut down those accounts, profiles, or services in your allotted time. Now that's productive computing working for you. (If you have extra time, then "unsubscribe" from all those spam e-mails you get as well. Don't wait for spring to clean that in-box!)

Now go back to that notebook and complete the next step (using a typical day from last week as a base):

++ For every twenty e-mails you send each day, add 2 points

++ For every ten texts you send each day, add
2 points

++ For every social-network update you make
each day, add 3 points

++ For every instant-message conversation you
have each day, add 3 points

++ For every fifteen minutes of cell-phone talk
time you use each day, add 2 points

Naturally, your VWI will go up. That's not the overarching concern. The problem arises with the content and the motivation. The *why* and the *what for*. Now take your VWI and commit it to memory. You don't have to share it with anyone. The purpose is to see your indulgence in technology in a way that makes it visual. Step back for a minute and really think about how many high-tech things are vying for your attention every day. It's a lot. And the number has crept up at a rapid pace. At the end of this Digital Diet you may choose to keep all those gadgets and services. That's fine. But you may alter how and when you use them. Just as with a food diet, you don't necessarily have to give up eating chocolate—you just don't down a whole cake every day. It's a cliché because it's true—

Exercise Day 4

Remember voice mail? I'm not talking about answering machines. I'm talking about the miraculous technology already in your smart phone that lets you receive an audio message. Yes! It's true. We've forgotten that smart phones are still phones. The next time you get a call and you're in the middle of dinner or shopping with your hands full of grocery bags or making a presentation at work—*don't answer it*. Obviously it's just rude to interrupt someone to reach for your device, but beyond that you're making yourself unnecessarily crazy. Let it go to voice mail. Record an outgoing message that asks people to leave a specific message and the time of the call. You'll get back to them *on your schedule*. Unless you know the call is urgent, just let it ring. I know people who have nearly killed themselves in a mad rush to answer a phone. Get your ducks in a row first, *then* answer it. Or call back later. It works. (It's better than crashing your car at the mall while trying to park.)

TechFact

According to an August 2010 Nielsen survey, the most text-happy states are Mississippi, Pennsylvania, Ohio, Oklahoma, Kansas, Wyoming, and Utah. Texters in these states averaged more than six hundred messages per month.

moderation, moderation, moderation. And nowhere is moderation more needed than in today's modern society.

Setting Social Limits

How, then, do we structure our intake of all the noise? This is from Twitter's site, in answer to a FAQ about whether it's all just too much information:

The result of using Twitter to stay connected with friends, relatives, and coworkers is that you have a sense of what folks are up to but you are not expected to respond to any updates

unless you want to. This means you can step
in and out of the flow of information as it suits
you and it never queues up with increasing
demand of your attention. Additionally, users
are very much in control of whose updates
they receive, when they receive them, and on
what device. For example, we provide settings
for scheduling Twitter to automatically turn
off at dinnertime and users can switch off
Twitter updates at any point. Simply put,
Twitter is what you make of it—receive a lot of
information about your friends, or just a tiny
bit. It's up to them.

Really? Because I can't find the scheduled Twitter
settings anywhere on its site.

Come on—how many people do you know who
minimize the frequency of their Twitter updates?
It's a nice idea, but we seem to crave the attention
and the opportunity that brevity, coupled with
broadcasting, provides. And when the "fail whale"
pops up, well, some people feel like they're drown-
ing. Decide today to use all the functionality of
Twitter if you must, but don't let it dictate your time.
First, consider your own scheduled tweets. Instead
of randomly posting all day, choose specific times to

send your messages—perhaps tied to meals, so after breakfast, lunch, and/or dinner. Maybe you only tweet on your laptop or desktop instead of on the go. And keep it to just a few minutes. Don't labor too long over those 140 characters—no one is giving you a grade on your Twitter skills. Also, don't be afraid of posting the equivalent of an out-of-office message, like "I won't be checking Twitter for a few days—best wishes." I'd highly recommend limiting the people you follow, too. Cluttering up your Twitter feed is a sure way to spend too much time sifting through mindless drivel.

If you're looking for a little software to help you out, try ManageFlitter, which is free—just go to ManageFlitter.com. From there, sign in to your Twitter account by clicking on the "start" button, and you'll be able to clean up the signal-to-noise ratio. ManageFlitter lets you trim who you follow, locate inactive accounts, and search your stream. It will even suggest who you should stop following to minimize the mess. For an even more stringent (and basic) approach, you could use a site like MinutesPlease.com. It will keep your Twitter (or any Web site) window open for the time that you allot (for example, ten minutes). After a one-minute warning, the window closes. Of course, you can al-

TechFact

A new study, published in the August 2010 issue of *Archives of Pediatrics and Adolescent Medicine*, followed 1,618 Chinese students between the ages of thirteen and eighteen. The study revealed that students who used the Internet pathologically (often for entertainment and games, not information) were 2.3 times more likely to develop depression, even if they had been free of mental-health problems prior to any Internet addiction. Lack of sleep was cited as one likely explanation.

ways open it again, but perhaps the shutdown will at least prompt you to move on.

Take Action: Recent studies have found that teenagers get better and more restful sleep after watching TV than after playing video games. This doesn't mean you should cut out the video games; it means you should recognize when they're becoming a problem by watching your teen's behavior. Every video-game console has settings to limit the amount of time it's used—get to know them. And be sure to set passwords so you're the only one in control.

iDisappeared

That online social-network activity requires an investment of time: logging in, perusing the profiles, deciding who deserves our interaction. Reading, updating, uploading. But over time, as we send a poke or a wall post or a virtual gift, this activity can generate negative value for our real center of being. I fell victim, wishing that those online missives meant more than they did. What was I getting in return? It was a quick fix that didn't amount to any lasting growth or development. That's the trap of social networks. They are set up to provide you with stimuli and voyeurism and an audience. We imagine that everyone in our network is benefiting from our pointing and clicking. But are they? Pause for second. Consider what it all really means. One of my wife's distant relatives would routinely post messages on my Facebook wall. To the casual observer, it might seem like I know her really well and we stay in touch and isn't she lovely. But I've never met her. My wife doesn't even speak with her. And over time it got really weird. She may be a perfectly wonderful person, but why was she so compelled to post these messages, and what was it accomplishing? Was it purely to satisfy her need to try to "keep the family together"? Was she lonely? Perhaps she was just being nice. But we have nothing in common, and if we ever found ourselves in the same room I wager that we'd probably feel awkward and not say anything. It's a bit bizarre, isn't it? Is there someone like that in your life? Or are you that person?

When I checked out of social networks, I could hear the groans of "What is wrong with this guy?" or "Grow up and stop whining about lack of inner strength." And in truth, if I had read this diatribe by someone like me in 2009, I would've dismissed him or her as self-serving and naive. But here's a question for you: Why don't you delete or deactivate your Facebook or MySpace or Twitter account? What's stopping you? How is it *improving* your life? When I tell people what I did, they sometimes recoil and then shrug and say, "Oh well, no big deal, I guess." So I suggest that they delete their social-network profiles. They shuffle their feet and say that seems too drastic. Perhaps. There are certainly other ways to come at your digital intake, and my mission is to make this approach manageable, customizable, and digestible. But don't ever be afraid to choose the "nuclear option" and walk away, at least for a while. It can be empowering.

Family Tip

Encourage the idea of "no-heads-down discussions" while in the house. No one is allowed to be looking down at a gadget or a computer while having a conversation. If your son or daughter (or husband or wife) won't take the time to make eye contact and look up while talking, then simply stop the conversation until they do. If a task needs to be done on a gadget or a computer, then it should be completed first and not done during a conversation. Keep the face-to-face chat sacrosanct. It won't be easy, and confrontations will surely occur, but try to be resolute in your enforcement.

Your Core

So what does it mean to be strong, to be persuasive? To reach people? To shape our behavior? Do social networks play a role in that? Of course they do. But before we had social networks there were clearly ways to get feedback from a group of other people and build self-confidence, though now we seem to have largely forgotten how to do that.

Social networks are designed to make you feel like they provide a positive, rewarding experience. Always. Why wouldn't they? That's their business model. If you joined a social network and ultimately felt like you weren't finding people or staying or touch or sharing your lives, then why would you stay on it? But I argue that the data out there (a) isn't being processed (e.g., people are not really reading Twitter feeds and are solely sending tweets out), (b) is often superficial and misleading, and (c) doesn't elicit more communication but rather can stunt any growth because of its closed-off nature (e.g., you read a status update or a Twitter feed and, rather than engage in a meaningful conversation with that person, simply respond with a short comment of your own).

At this point I must reiterate that I am not advocating the dismantling of social networks. They can serve a mighty role in creating a community, from finding loved ones to surviving a disaster like the earthquake in Haiti to providing a rallying cry such as the Twitter-influenced groundswell in Iran. But social networks do not thrive because of an oc-

casional world event or tragedy. They thrive because
of our increasing interest in promoting ego online.
They offer themselves as a way to stay in touch with
others and tell people what you're doing and generally bring people closer to you. In fact, they are in
many ways doing exactly the opposite. By and large
we have become indolent shouters. It sounds harsh,
but there's no way around it. Use the Digital Diet to

Exercise Day 5

Clear your status update and don't type
anything for the duration of the day. You're
still allowed to read Facebook updates, as
long as you keep within the limit of your diet,
but refrain from posting anything yourself.
Of course, you can still share those bursts of
observations with those you know and love—
just try doing it in a different manner. Pick
up the phone and call them. Write a short
e-mail. Even text. Anything that creates
a direct connection. (If you don't have a
Facebook account, then same goes for any
social network, like MySpace or LinkedIn
or others.)

remember what it really means to be in touch. And don't let social networks become your primary place for family communication—a few friends of mine use it to learn what their kids are up to, as in, "I have no idea what my daughter is doing until I read her status update." Sure, you can add your kids on Facebook and follow them on Twitter. But nothing will replace that face-to-face time.

Inner Voices

Ayn Rand encouraged us to think for ourselves and adhere to our own morality. She believed that no one should sacrifice themselves and do something for someone else simply because they felt any peer pressure related to altruism. What would Rand make of social networks? It's an interesting conundrum. On the one hand, you have people serving their own self-interest and enhancing their own ego with glorious status updates and amazing photos. On the other hand, we've become a nation of followers. Our sense of unique self is being eroded by our desire to get people to click on the "like" button beneath our status updates or receive cheery comments below a photo or receive yet another "friend request."

Rand never meant for people to live alone or eschew human contact. But we've found a way to live both alone and together. And I'm easily one of the worst examples. At some point in our digital evolution, many of us traded privacy for ego. What I mean is that it became more intriguing, more tantalizing, to reveal ourselves (or how we imagine ourselves) to the rest of the world than to internalize our lives a bit more or share them with an immediate sphere of people.

In the virtual world we can receive a broad spectrum of feedback and approval and encouragement in a brief period of time in a way that's simply not possible in the real one. And it's worth noting that privacy is not the same thing as secrecy. What we deem unfit for public consumption may still be something we share with our closest (real-life) friend. But our avatar or alter ego sees social networks as a chance to feel justified or accepted or vindicated. And if you think your social-network profile doesn't exemplify some of those tendencies, then go through your list of friends and count how many you see on a regular basis or know really well or have ever met in person. Why do they each receive the same sentiments? Evenly distributing your communication isn't always best.

Family Tip

Spend part of a day rounding up your family's printed photographs. Put everyone to work in the search. The photos might be in drawers, in boxes under the bed, or attached to the fridge with a magnet. Once you've got as many as you can find, work together to organize them into groups: friends, family, and events. On the back of each photo, write down the event and date and identify the people, just like your parents did.

After you've sorted them, use some of your allotted online time to visit ScanMyPhotos.com or FotoBridge.com. For a relatively small fee (about five cents per photo) these services will scan your photos at a high resolution and send them back to you on a DVD. A trip down memory lane with a reward at the end.

Your E-buddy

There are a number of services that can force you to consciously manage time spent on the computer and help trim your VWI. I'd like you to explore at least one of them.

RescueTime: The most notable is a downloadable program called RescueTime. Its purpose is to divide your time into sections and channel your energy in a linear fashion. To do that, it takes over your computer or laptop in some ways. For example, if you're working on an accounting report, it will allow you to have access to an Excel spreadsheet but not the Web. You can't mindlessly surf the latest entertainment gossip instead of drilling down into the returns on investment. It's a bit like shackling yourself to your task, but the point is that we all need a bit of that. The negative byproduct of multitasking—whether you believe in its effectiveness or not—is that it often leads to distraction. Some say those diversions open gateways in the brain, while others say they make us forget why we started working in the first place. RescueTime is a bit like an intervention. It steps in and says, "Put away the mouse for a while—focus on the keyboard." And it rewards you along the way. The software is designed to track your progress and give you feedback on how well you used your time. Rescuing your time could mean rescuing your sanity in the long run. Here now is a first-person account of RescueTime from my friend Porter Anderson:

It gives you hard, cold knowledge about what
you're actually doing online, right down to the
seconds you spend on it. If you've ever started
weighing yourself again after a while, or
hooked a pedometer to your shorts when you
go out for a walk, then you know why this is
important. We're all liable to fall into the trap
of thinking "Hey, that sour cream last night
was fat-free" or "Hey, I'm running at least five
miles every morning," only to find out that
the fat-free sour cream has let us down and the
run is actually two miles, not five.

At this point, I recommend going to RescueTime
.com and downloading its small background program (for Mac or PC). It will seamlessly start tracking the active application or program or site, second
by second. Here's more from Anderson on its effectiveness:

The developers call it "automagical tracking,"
but it's going to feel like pretty black magic
the first time you log into your RescueTime
dashboard and discover the e-mail you
thought you spent 25 minutes on? Two hours,
14 minutes. That quick check to see if Amazon

.com had the book you were looking for? Thirty-four minutes. Those three tweets you read from friends, and answered, then had to answer back when all three friends answered you and retweeted all over the place? . . . Ah, Twitter, you just ate up 56 more minutes of my day. Yes, every single thing you've done on your computer is there. Everything. You'll be shocked and awed. Without the RescueTime dashboard, most of us can't recall a fraction of what we've done and where we've been in a day, a week, a month, a year. RescueTime breaks it all down into whatever time increments you want and lays it all out for you in really informative, easy-to-read bar graphs and lists.

But here's where it gets even better: your inner empire gets to strike back. RescueTime's listings of the various sites and apps you've been using (or have they been using you?) come with ratings based on other users' rankings—anywhere from Very Productive to Very Distracting. You can then adjust those ratings for your personal situation. Can't stand that blog by the guy who compares everything he does to a scene from some movie? Set him to Very Distracting. Love that site with the

recipes that leave out one crucial ingredient
you have to guess? Set it to Very Productive.
The most powerful tool is called Get Focused.
This will block anything you've rated Very
Distracting for exactly the number of minutes
you want. So if you just need to get the instant
messages and Facebook notifications out
of your hair and spend 10 minutes on an
important report before a meeting, set Focus
Mode for 10 minutes.

Another feature, project tracking, gives you
the ability to credit yourself with time offline,
too. Say you've done some reading or phoning
or legwork on a project and you'd like to get
that time credited to your pet project but of
course the computer has no idea what you've
been up to. You just jump to your projects and
drag them into precisely the time you've spent,
and there you have it, a full online and offline
accounting of what you've been doing. You can
even get into it as a family—a special tour is
there for the clan that wants to skinny down
together on excess digital consumption.

Slife: A similar program is called Slife. Once you
sign up for the program online (the Plus version

monitors up to five activities, while the Premium version is unlimited), you can view your Web profile anytime with a detailed overview of your wired time. Slife breaks it down into categories like "reading tech news" and provides a stark, inescapable look at your own "pie chart" of online activity. You can also use a virtual "egg timer" to manage your various demands, so you could set fifteen minutes for reading your daily dose of Gawker and TMZ, while you notch it up a bit for TechCrunch, Slashdot, and Lifehacker (or *Women's Wear Daily* or *Slate* or whatever your interest may be). What's also great about Slife is that it's partnered with FreshBooks, which helps with project billing. So as a self-employed person, you could use Slife to automatically measure the time you spend on different companies and then seamlessly bill it all based on the time. So while there's no more lying to yourself about all that "research," a little exploratory Web browsing can help stimulate the creative juices. Slife also allows you to make notes and qualify why you ventured where you did. Between RescueTime and Slife, you will never view your Internet/computer interaction the same way again.

Saavi Accountability: Beyond the programs that control your technology addiction by being either offline or controlling time online is another offering called Saavi Accountability. It's more personal than the others and arguably more challenging. Instead of blocking or restricting access, it uses relationships to instill accountability. In other words, you choose an "accountability partner" who, with your permission, is notified when any questionable browsing takes place or there are attempts to circumvent the software. Allowing someone else to monitor your online life is a big step, but if your obsession with or addiction to technology is great, then it may be hugely beneficial to let someone in to help. The software records and reports when any addictive behavior is detected (a long time spent on a site, more time than allotted spent on a service), and it can be customized to monitor use of a particular site, like YouTube, or a particular category, like gambling. It can even go deeper by monitoring keywords within certain sites. It doesn't stop anyone from clicking on them; it's simply meant to watch the behavior and report and record it. It's a bit like having someone look over your shoulder, and over time it's meant to get easier as the user addresses the motivations and desires behind the behavior through talking with their partner. It also encourages parents to get involved with their kids' behavior and have discussions about why they might be tempted to go online or spend too much time on certain sites.

There can be a monthly fee for these types of aids, but it's hard to put a price on improved clarity and real connectivity. As we've started to see, technology can offer solutions, too, and we'll get into that much more in the coming chapters.

Forge ahead.

6

Surveying the Damage

Days 6–8

"The means by which we live have outdistanced the ends for which we live. Our scientific power has outrun our spiritual power. We have guided missiles and misguided men."

—**Dr. Martin Luther King, Jr.**

It's now time to reintroduce more of your devices and services into your daily routine as we take a close look at your current dependency situation, get you to ask yourself more hard questions (and answer honestly), and survey how we've all been caught up in the "latest and greatest." Even as you dabble in online life again, these few days will also be a time to focus on the need to keep a personal journal and engage in introspection rather than constantly broadcasting everything online. I'll encourage you to break free from your digital shell, start some offline hobbies, like cooking more with loved ones, and find ways to fill the void trimming technology leaves in your life.

Take Action: For days six, seven, and eight you can use any of your devices or services for a total of a one-hour e-day. Keep a record in your notebook of the amount of time spent on each one. Notice how your usage adds up and remember to think about why you're using each device or program. Are you picking up your smart phone to check sports scores? Are you texting because you don't want to return a phone call? How long are you roaming the Internet without a purpose? Certain applications and uses are perfectly acceptable and worth your time in the digital world. Others, not so much. Stay aware.

Ask Yourself: Each night during this phase, write about at least one of these questions in your daily journal. If your family's on the diet, try to discuss one of the questions around the dinner table or during some family downtime.

> What am I worried about losing if I minimize my dependence on technology and gadgets?

> In an ideal world, what would I like to get out of streamlining my high-tech intake?

> Has technology replaced something in my life that concerns me?

> Do I feel as though my identity is being shaped significantly by the Web and social networks?

> How and why does technology make my life better?

Now, ask yourself how the last few days have been without as much technology in your life.

> Have you felt isolated?

> Are you feeling more confident or more introspective?

> Are you afraid that the world has moved on without you?

> Do you see your immediate surroundings in a new light?

Have you tried to rekindle relations with family
members and make a concerted effort to
be aware of when technology tugs at your
attention?

None of these questions is necessarily easy to
address. And there are no wrong answers—only
missed opportunities to delve deeper into your personal situation. Likely it's a mix of many emotions,
some fairly intense, which should also demonstrate
the powerful place of technology in our lives.

As we've partly discussed, one of the greatest
digital time sucks for people of all ages is social networking: Facebook, Twitter, MySpace, LinkedIn.
Pick your poison. Since this aspect of online life mo-
nopolizes many people's time, let's take a minute to
examine social networks a little more deeply. Social
networking now consumes twice as much of our
online time as any other activity. According to research from Nielsen, sites like Facebook and Twitter
now account for nearly a quarter of time spent on
the Web; the next-closest activity is online games,
which make up about 10 percent. So how did we
get here? Did you join MySpace because it allowed
you to connect with people you'd forgotten about?
Why did you want them back in your life? Did you

join Facebook because it let you keep in touch better with friends and family? Were they complaining before 2007? Why fill a void that didn't exist? Yes, we can find out instantaneously about people's lives. But the truth is that personal interaction changed from one-on-one time to a drive-through connection. The more people joined, the easier it became to shrug off the reluctance of joining.

And it's affecting many corners of society. According to an Associated Press article from September 2010, the entire student body of eight hundred students at Harrisburg University of Science and Technology was banned from using social networks

TechFact

In a Nielsen survey in August 2010, women reported spending about 22 percent more time chatting on mobile phones than men did. They spent about 856 minutes per month on the line, on average, compared with 667 minutes for men. Women also texted more, sending or receiving an average of 601 texts per month, compared with 447 for men.

Re: Boot

on campus for a week. The dean said it was an experiment to get people to rethink their dependence on social networks and how technology has infiltrated our lives. The point, much like that of this Digital Diet, was to instill awareness and create a discussion. I must say, although the experiment offered no long-term strategy for the students, at least it got people talking. Even other schools took notice, according to the Associated Press report: "Do we really want to be enslaved to Facebook or Twitter?" said Sherrie Madia, communications director for the University of Pennsylvania's Wharton School. "Once you create anything in social media, you have to feed the beast. When you stop adding content,

Exercise Day 6

Write down one of your favorite memories that doesn't involve technology. Whatever it is, take the time to relive it through the words you put down on the page. Think about the aspects of it that you enjoyed and why it was so meaningful. It doesn't have to be an epic story; just focus on the tangible and rewarding parts.

you disappear." (For a while, that can be a good thing.) Well, guess what? The results came in after a week, and many students reported that while it was difficult, it did provide a chance to step back and see how they were spending, and wasting, their time.

My Facebook Vortex

Signing up on Facebook has a snowball effect, and nothing draws a crowd like a crowd. We each ask the same initial questions, like "Why would I share all this stuff with people?" Then we laugh nervously and look at one another and go ahead and do it anyway. There is safety in numbers, and social networks make our concerns seem more trivial and our achievements more significant.

When I signed up in April 2007, it was because I had been exposed in a dramatic way to the power of Facebook and MySpace to help grieve and unite. Virginia Tech was gripped by fear when a lone gunman, Seung-Hui Cho, brazenly and brutally killed thirty-two people and injured or terrorized dozens, hundreds, even thousands more. That day I was working in New York at the *CBS Evening News with Katie Couric*, and as the news broke I reached out to whomever I could find within the Virginia Tech community. But I didn't have a Facebook account, so I relied on sending e-mail to addresses available on the Web site of the student paper, *Planet Blacksburg*, which was providing updates to the outside world and serving as a lifeline to those wondering what was happening on campus. I ended up doing a webcam interview with one of the students who worked at *Planet Blacksburg* and later in the week did a story on how Facebook provided a place to express emotions and share memories. It became a virtual memorial, a place where students could open up to one another, no matter where they were in the country; the tragedy crossed borders and instilled a need to reach out for support. Facebook offered that service on a personal and a global level.

Before that exposure to it, I hadn't understood why I would want, or need, a Facebook page. And as a TV "personality" I worried about revealing too much. But there was no turning back once I signed up and saw how easily connections could be made. It's funny to look back upon, because I followed a now-established pattern of behavior that's shared by millions:

1. Question why I'd bother joining.

2. Sign up with limited personal information

exposed, and fill in the parts about "favorite movies" and "hobbies" and "quotes."

3. Upload one or two photos from recent events that had good lighting.

4. Search for former girlfriends/classmates.

5. "Friend" a series of people from past jobs, schools, and relationships, and then eventually sit back and wonder if that was such a good idea.

6. Get a flattering comment or wall post and find a few friends.

7. Extol the virtues of Facebook to everyone I know and encourage them to join, too.

But a national tragedy that brought people together was in many ways the beginning of my own personal relations coming apart. I fell into the rabbit hole of social networks and couldn't find my way out; the importance of my online life often surpassed that of my real one. Indeed, I set off on the experiment that inspired this book (deactivating my social networks for several months) with the hope of killing my alter ego and boosting my real-life social connections. The experiment also spurred me to examine what privacy means to me and whether I am better off with a closed loop. Once I shut off my digital broadcasts, did I really want to turn them back on? I have begun to feel better about not sharing my life and my thoughts in such a public manner as social networks. I'm more focused on what's actually happening and what it means to me and those I love. While I'm back on Facebook to a limited degree, I don't let it define me. I share work-related information (and, yes, self-promotion) and occasionally use it as a place to post a few photos of my daughter for friends and family. To a lesser degree I also use LinkedIn, which is a social network geared more toward the business crowd. There I mainly offer updates on my work endeavors and try to "network" in the old-fashioned sense of the word (circa 2005). But I resist the urge to let it define me or shape me. I want people to know me in real life and only get snippets online.

That said, it's been hard at times. I occasionally get what I call "social network echoes"—something happens in my life and I catch myself formulating how I'd write a status update or a tweet. When I pause and reflect, it seems stupid and trivial, yet I used to obsess about it every day. Lately I try not to surf around other people's Facebook pages too much unless they're close friends or family. I've also realized that I have a harder time remembering some people's names if I can't occasionally log in for a refresher. But then I think—if I can't remember their names, then maybe they aren't really *in* my life. It's kind of like that rule about giving away clothes you haven't worn for more than a year. I mean, at some point, if you aren't actually saying your friend's name out loud anymore, are they still your friend? Look deeper into your social networks and see what turns up. Are there friends whose names you haven't said out loud of late?

Family Tip

Schedule a time for the entire household's gadgets to be charged. In other words, let's say at around 9:00 p.m. all the gadgets use the same power bar or charging station in the house. The gadgets get to hang out together while the family members turn their attention to other things (or preferably one another).

The People Meter

No one, certainly not I, will deny that today's pace of life requires that we communicate with people through less face-to-face time. We're on the go, we're trying to manage our lives, and we're just not able to slow down as much as we'd like to and engage in a more personal fashion. There are questions about how this type of interaction is shaping a whole new generation, and studies have shown that one of the great shifts involves the loss of "social niceties." Younger people simply don't have the time or patience for the "Hi, how are you?" "Fine, and you?" moments. They prefer to get right to the point, and technology (especially texting) allows that. In fact, you could blame wireless companies for killing the casual greeting, since limiting text messages to the essentials means paying less money. (And since so many multitaskers are craving information, they can cut right to the chase.)

Family Tip

A family that blogs together stays together. At least it can't hurt. To create a family blog site, start at a place like Blogspot.com or MyFamily.com. From there you and the kids can upload photos, share a calendar, and keep track of extended family members. (It's also a great way to include the grandparents.) A few safety rules to keep in mind: (1) be sure to set the preferences to "private" so only you can decide who gets to view your content; (2) err on the side of caution and don't display too much personal information, like a physical home address (also consider using only first names, not last); and (3) set the photos so someone can't right-click and download them (most sites offer that option). Bottom line: be creative!

So why blather on in person? It's true, face-to-face conversation is free but certainly more time-consuming. Yet what concerns me is when "chat shift" occurs. That's when you start a relationship with a friend or colleague and spend much of your time in person but then migrate to instant messages. Or you only use e-mail with your family members and no longer pick up the phone. What happens and why? Sometimes it's almost imperceptible (and can be based on things like schedules and distance), yet we often get a sense that something has indeed changed.

Take Action: Here's the test: Grab some writing material and draw three columns. Head the first column "in person," the second "in writing," and the third "via voice." Over the course of a few days,

Exercise Day 7

Tonight, make a mental or physical note of the places you reached for your gadgets. Was it when you were alone or when you were with others? Was it because of a lull in conversation, or were you bored? Did you do it several times over the course of ten to fifteen minutes? Did anyone around you make a comment about it? Begin to pay attention to the settings and not just what you say in your messages. These are the times when your head (and your data) is in the "clouds." In the future, the next time you're at a restaurant and someone goes to the bathroom, resist the urge to pick up your device. Look around at the people eating and see how many are typing away on their keypads and touch

in the first column put the people in your life with whom you interacted in person (i.e., close enough to smell their breath). In the second put the people with whom you chatted via phone or Skype or webcam. And in the third put the people you interacted with through written means like e-mail or texts or screens. It's a revealing sight. Instead, let your mind cycle through its concerns like a roulette wheel. Stop on a particular problem. Behavioral psychologist Katherine Muller would like us to use that occasion to tolerate an emotion and feel the need to really feel it. Then when the person returns to the table, bring up your thoughts (if appropriate) and vocalize what was bugging you. The key, says Muller, is to deal with those nagging feelings in the immediate present using conversation and human contact. Be mindful of your own situation and remove yourself from the isolation that's offered by your device. It all goes back to enlisting those around you as a support group and remembering the limitless benefits of face-to-face contact.

instant messages. You may begin to see a pattern develop.

Are there people with whom you exchange e-mails but whom you miss talking to? Have you lumped your relatives into the written category and never call them anymore? Is it time to set up a real date

TechFact

Ten percent of people twenty-four and younger think it's okay to text during sex, according to consumer-electronics shopping and review site Retrevo.

with someone you only see on Skype? Does it feel like you're pushing some people aside for the sake of convenience? The People Meter is meant to gauge over time how your interactions shift and why. It's about tracking not just where the people fall in each column but why they appear there. Consider whether you're intentionally compartmentalizing people and segregating them, or whether it's really a matter of necessity. Ask yourself the hard questions—only you have the answers.

Compressing Time

Imagine the deadlines and demands in our lives as circular ripples extending out beyond us. Each person or job or setting puts different demands on our time. But because we can reach out to anyone anywhere in the world at any time, we've started to "compress time." Those ripples lack definition and strength. They collapse on one another and make us think we can't wait longer to respond or get back to someone. I'm very guilty of this. I'm one of those people who absolutely must get something done or I worry that I will forget about it later. One morning as we walked the dog, my wife asked me to check on something. She didn't say to do it right then. But I pulled out my phone and began to look up the information (the date that a mutual acquaintance was scheduled to return to the office after a holiday). She scoffed and scolded me for interrupting our walk. I agreed. It was a knee-jerk reaction because I thought I wouldn't remember to do such a relatively minor task down the road. A better idea might've been to ask her to remind me later. Trust that you'll gravitate back to the problem. You could also use your device to make a quick note, explain to the person what you're doing, and then follow up later. On a larger scale, we see projects due well into the future and forget that we really do have a lot of time to accomplish them. But thanks to gadgets and the Web breaking down barriers, we've lost sight of the true rigidity of time. Time is on our side if we ally ourselves with it. That means looking at each hour and not squishing the minutes and seconds down to nothing. Respect the minutes and seconds.

Family Tip

Create a contest within the family for the least amount of texting. It's easy to tally—just use the monthly bill(s). Set a decent but inexpensive reward tailored to each family member (e.g., new barbecue tools for dad, new shoes for daughter) and see who wins. The cost savings on the texts isn't so much the issue. Remember: It's not about being out of touch. It's about maximizing those texts and making them meaningful. Reduce the mindless texting. No one should lose any friends during the contest—on the contrary, it might bring everyone a little closer together.

Do I Really Need This Gadget?

Speaking of gadgets, if you own a high-tech device of any kind, then you probably have a favorite store at which you purchase technology. It could be Best Buy or Fry's Electronics or Dave's Doodads. I don't care and it doesn't matter. I'm not saying not to go there again—in fact, just the opposite. Here's your challenge: The next time you are near that store, go in and look around as you might do anyway. Make a mental list of all the gadgets you'd love to have. Has that list changed at all since you started the dietary approach? Are you considering gadgets with a more practical nature over ones that provide more flash? If so, reward yourself with a little extra e-mail time.

Technology manufacturers have long used ploys to lure people in to buying the next new thing. So why do we capitulate? Often it can be peer pressure. Early adopters love getting "stuff" and trying it out. And sometimes we really think that the next version will improve upon the problems with the first one. Sure, I love to talk about technology and gadgets on TV or in print, and I'm often impressed by the cool stuff out there (also occasionally unimpressed by the slew of junk). But while I get products sent to me, I eventually send them all back and buy only the ones I need (most of the time). Ultimately, the best approach in a dietary sense is to consider the nutritional benefits; we all fall off the healthy bandwagon once in a while, but we should do our best to choose the right foods.

Let me give you a quick personal example: When the Apple iPad came out, I couldn't possibly imagine where it'd fit in my life. Virtually all of the ads featured someone lying on their back and resting the iPad on their knees. Seriously, when are you *ever* in that position? And the form function seemed wholly impractical to me—typing on a virtual keyboard *and* finding a flat surface on which to do it? I didn't get it, so I didn't buy it. But Apple did offer a loaner iPad. So I thought, "Why not? I'll check it out." Well, sure enough, I was right. I couldn't find a time or reason to use it. But my wife did. During the course of her pregnancy she clung to the iPad like a lifeline. It was light, portable, and perfect for a pregnant woman who did spend a lot of her time lying on her back resting the iPad on her knees. A home run. But the next time you visit a store filled with shiny objects, ask yourself (or get the person next to you to ask): Is this gadget helping me stay better in touch? Will it cause further distraction in my life? And can I really afford to buy it? Look, I've always loved cool stuff. If you're even modestly into technology, then you can relate. But begin questioning whether you need it. Will it improve your life? Of course we all buy stuff we don't need, but examine your decisions more closely. Don't get caught in the hype cycle of version this and that. Not only will you feel like a stronger consumer, but you'll also save some money.

Don't Be a Data Hoarder

There are many tragic (and extreme) examples of people who can't throw out a single possession. They live in squalor and filth and often die in that environment. Dealing with something as simple as an old sweater turns into an enormous ordeal. We pity them and wish they could learn to separate "the thing" from the emotion or "the thing" from the person. All too often "the things" take precedence because "the things" don't talk back or give them grief or cause alarm. But in the twenty-first century there is a new category of this type of obsessive-compulsive behavior—data hoarding.

Yet we have all become digital pack rats. We have so many digital photos and e-mails we want to save, and with no single place to keep them, we don't end up deleting anything. We fret over whether we'll still have this laptop ten years from now or whether a certain format could be read by computers as our grandkids grow up. Or we simply don't want to delete those e-mails that built a relationship. My wife actually printed out the majority of the e-mails and instant messages that we exchanged while courting in 2001. Yes, I was the shy (aka nerdy) coworker who started the come-hither messages. And while I'm all about saving trees, there was something oddly reassuring about having tangible copies of these irreplaceable moments of our history. I don't think either of us still have any digital traces of these steamy conversations (it's a fun read), but I'm not overly worried since we have the scrapbook.

We are going to continue to face this conundrum, as our entire lives are increasingly lived out online. We don't just have e-mails and instant messages; we have text messages and Facebook posts and terabytes of digital video and photos that build up over time. We buy new external hard drives to accommodate them and attempt to purge some items. We get more space in our Gmail account and forward everything to the "cloud." And we rarely print stuff out anymore, since it's time-consuming and soooooooo 2003. Therefore, we've all started to exhibit some minor tendencies of a "data hoarder."

Muller has studied a spectrum of these types of personalities (a subset of obsessive-compulsive disorder) and attempts to treat them with an extreme type of Digital Diet. Muller believes in "acceptance and commitment" therapy—in other words, getting information hoarders to address their reliance on saving everything and proceed to a place in their life that puts it in perspective. And while the vast majority of us aren't "hoarders," we may still keep too much stuff in our in-box or text-message queue or cache. If you eliminate the unnecessary messages and e-crap that are kicking around your various devices, you may actually find it lifts a burden from your brain. Like a mini cleanse. Every time you open those applications it will seem more empowering when you aren't bogged down by digital leftovers.

Take Action: Use some of your online time to hit the delete key, and feel the weight lift off your shoulders. Open your e-mail in-box and review messages from the last few weeks. If it isn't essential in your life or critical to save, then delete it. I challenge you to get your in-box down below five to ten unread items. Look at what those messages are saying or doing: Are they reminders? Sentimental? Things you don't want to deal with? Use your online time wisely and tackle as many as you can. Easier said than done, of course, like a lot of things worth doing. But perhaps we can all learn something from those information hoarders before it's too late.

Your E-buddy: If you need a little e-assistance, then look into a service called Inbox Zero. It

TechFact

The Kaiser Family Foundation found in 2010 that about 50 percent of students from eight to eighteen were using the Internet, watching TV, or using some other form of media either "most" (31 percent) or "some" (25 percent) of the time that they were doing homework.

encourages you to improve your "e-mail fu" by tackling e-mails in a timely and efficient fashion. Rather than letting them fester and annoy you and turn into fungus, brush them into a folder or dash out a worthy response. It's about a cohesive system for folders, filters, and nonstop messages so your in-box is a place of reward rather than refuge.

Line of Site

In October 2009 two Kansas State University researchers released their findings about the importance of peripheral vision. You might think it had to do with defending our primal selves from attackers and making sure no enemy crept up on us. That may be true, but they also noted that peripheral vision was important for the brain to perceive our surroundings. In essence, it puts what our eyes are seeing in context. They showed subjects two different images—one with the center obscured and one with the periphery obscured. They found that the subjects were better able to identify the content of the image when the center was obscured. Therefore, the researchers said, even though our eyes move about three times per second, we're able to absorb a quick hit of information in that time that provides us with greater understanding. But take away the center and we lose the perspective.

These days, I can't help but wonder if that loss of

Exercise Day 8

Set all your gadgets to vibrate, turn down the volume on your laptop or computer, and turn off any alerts or alarms. The point is to go silent for a while. Minimize the additional noise from technology just for a day and see if it makes you a little less agitated and anxious. You'll still be in touch.

perspective is occurring while we walk from place to place. Consider the last time you pulled out your smart phone or cell phone and started texting or e-mailing or instant messaging someone as you walked. Your peripheral vision likely dipped down to zero as you focused solely on the task at hand. You compromised the key to your survival: dodging any oncoming pedestrians (and parking meters or light poles) and ensuring the light was really green when you stepped forward. I've done it myself on more occasions than I care to admit. But I've become hyper-aware of it and try to stop shortly after I begin. Not only is it unsafe, but it also looks pretty self-absorbed and silly to those around you/me. When was the last time you walked any great distance and resisted the urge to fire off a missive? I'll admit, it's not easy. Walking can be the only time available to quickly catch up on e-mails or texts. But we're missing the periphery. And as our brains tell us, the periphery gives us context. That vertical navigation as we move forward is turning us into gophers—tunneling ahead with little regard for what's in front of us. On the other hand, a koala is perhaps the exact opposite, lingering in one spot for hours at a time and munching away on those eucalyptus leaves. Maybe the happy medium is a fox, fleet of foot and moving with confidence, but also acutely aware of every creature nearby. Consider being the fox more than the gopher (or the koala, even though they're insufferably cute). Besides, foxes are known to eat gophers. Don't be afraid of eye contact—it still means something.

Keep that notebook handy and ruminate on your answers to the tough questions. Next: technology's many benefits. (Plus plenty of tricks to impress your friends and family members!)

Step 3

Re: Connect

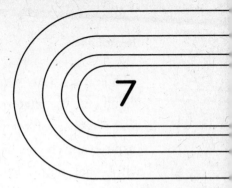

7

Mind and Body Dexterity 2.0

Days 9–11

"Every two days, we create as much information as we did up to 2003."

—Eric Schmidt, CEO of Google, August 2010

Adapting to life in the twenty-first century means constantly learning new
skills and programs and gadgets. But flexing those
newfound muscles can make us weary and keeping up with an onslaught of information can be

exhausting. To say we're overwhelmed is an understatement. The purpose of this chapter is to arm you with physical and mental exercises to challenge and inspire you. The benefit of these exercises and apps will be not just in developing any lost strength but also in helping fill the void of technology and build new (beneficial) habits. Embrace the ones that work and at least give most of them a try.

Your E-day: At this stage of the Digital Diet you can begin using your devices and services for a total of ninety minutes per e-day. Remember to keep up that awareness—think about the "why" when you turn to them. Do it for the right reasons. I hope you're beginning to feel more empowered at this point! Just don't forget to pace yourself.

Balls and Bands

During an early brainstorming session while formulating this diet, I considered suggesting that people put all their devices in a couple of pillowcases and use them as dumbbells. Alas, I worry this will only result in scratched screens and personal-injury lawsuits. So let's go with something else.

Repeated use of gadgets and keyboards can easily result in carpal tunnel syndrome. Even if you don't get an extreme case of it, the aching and pain can be debilitating. I've had it to a lesser degree myself, mainly in my thumbs, thanks to holding my iPhone with one hand and typing that way.

This first exercise is pretty basic but helps prevent carpal tunnel, so it's an important one. And all you need is a tennis ball. You only need one tennis ball, but you can use two if you want to work both of your hands at the same time. Hold your arm out from your body with your palm facing down, tennis ball in your hand. Squeeze the ball fifteen to twenty times per hand. Then take a break. Repeat.

Repeat that sequence for about five to ten minutes a day and you will soon notice a distinct improvement in your hands—reduced strain and improved flexibility. It's not complicated, but it works, and you can even do it while reading or watching a DVD or texting (kidding).

Another great hand exercise is to stretch an elastic band over your fingers and expand and contract them like a drunken starfish. This will help you regain some dexterity in your fingers. Just fifteen to twenty repetitions per hand over about five to ten minutes and you'll be on your way to dexterous digits for your digital pursuits.

Take Action: Invest in a pedometer and try to work yourself up to taking ten thousand steps a day. These days pedometers are very cheap, and you can even get them as an app for your smart phone (there are dozens of them in the iTunes store alone). Carve out that time for exercise and you'll find yourself getting a much-needed boost mentally and physically.

Exercise Day 9

This is a chapter full of exercises, but there are still general ones that should be done each day. In this case, I want you to observe. Find a window and just watch what happens on the street or in the park, or simply let your gaze wander. This can be a great way to clear your head before diving back into the next task. It sounds simplistic, and it is. But many times we don't do the simple things, and as a result our lives become more complicated. For about five to ten minutes today just let your eyes be your guide and zone out a bit.

You don't need to be militant about it, but it's part of enhancing your awareness going forward.

Mental Gymnastics

A slew of studies have found that keeping the mind sharp and energized can infuse brain cells with more power and even stave off the likes of Alzheimer's disease. I encourage you to test out as many of these apps and programs as you want to see which ones work the best for you. The purpose is to improve your brainpower and mental agility using technology—so long as it doesn't cut into time spent in real life with loved ones and friends. Balance! Some programs are designed more for people on the go, while others are aimed at those in a solitary and quiet place. It won't hurt to try.

Crosswords, sudoku, Scrabble (iPhone, Android, BlackBerry, and Windows Mobile 7 devices): Word-association and number games are among the most effective types of mental exercises out there. Thanks to the rising popularity of apps and smart phones, it's easy to get many of the classic puzzles of your childhood on your mobile device and use them on the train or bus or waiting at an airport. Check them out—super easy. Many are listed as the title would suggest (crossword, sudoku, etc.), but others are more unique and grouped together. For example, PuzzleManiak ($1.99, iPhone), offers twenty puzzles in one app, ranging from visual challenges to classic games. There's also Brain Teaser of the Day (iPhone), which offers 365 different logic puzzles (great for challenging the kids, too).

Brain Age (Nintendo DS series): One of the most popular games for all ages on the Nintendo DS handheld device is Brain Age. Using the stylus, you solve all kinds of puzzles, from math problems to letter scrambles to currency counting. It was inspired by the work of prominent Japanese neuroscientist Dr. Ryuta Kawashima. Though Nintendo makes no claim about the scientific benefits of Brain Age, it's one of the best brain-building games out there. The hard part can be when it suggests your brain is older than you are!

BrainTeaser (iPhone): At first glance this game looks pretty easy, but it's actually both stimulating and frustrating (in a way that makes you want to overcome it). The game presents a group of squares within a large rectangle. Each square is one of two colors. When you tap on a square it changes to the other color, as do its neighbors, thereby creating a new design. At the bottom is the pattern you must achieve; your goal is to change the appropriate squares to match that design. It's harder than it sounds and definitely flexes the brain muscles.

Braingle (iPhone, iPod, iPad): Braingle brings together a number of visual and written puzzles, as well as optical illusions, riddles, and logic problems. The company claims to have more than fifteen thousand mental exercises available, with more added every day to "tangle" your brain. This one is also free, but some folks complain about the number of ads. However, since it's free, it's worth just trying it.

Cup O' Joe (iPhone, iPod, iPad): This app costs $1.99 but claims to include many clever ways to fire up your brain in the morning. You can train across many levels and keep track of your progress. Some catchy background music accompanies you as a rapid-fire series of questions (math, trivia) force you to respond and wake up that problem-solving cortex. There's even a music-based one that involves memorizing the treble and bass clefs. But don't necessarily give up coffee. At least not because I said so.

Freedom From Stress (iPhone): This aptly named app was designed by Stephan Bodian, who wrote *Meditation for Dummies*. It's a way to untangle your mind a bit, review your stress indicators, and practice ways to cut down your anxiety. It costs a bit more than most, at $4.99, but claims to offer "scientifically proven" strategies. There are others, too, that are part of a series offered by Mental Workout, the company that makes Freedom From Stress. For $9.99 you can get a number of apps that deal with everything from jet lag to meditation to happiness. There is a Web-based group of programs, too, for those of you not into mobile apps.

iThoughtsHD (iPad): Organizing our daily ideas and lists can be a never-ending struggle. But what if you could visualize them and maybe prioritize everything through a kind of "mind-mapping" process? That's the idea behind iThoughtsHD, which gets you to lay out your inner monologue in black and white (and some colors). The software looks for patterns and tries to inspire you to tackle each project or concern with an organized approach. It looks kind of like a tree diagram or a series of rabbit warrens. The color coding is meant to denote different categories of thought (green for creativity, red for feeling) and show you the connected ones. It's one of the more expensive apps, at $9.99, but it might really help put things in perspective. There is nothing like seeing your scattered thoughts all laid out in front of you.

Exercise Day 10

It's time to tackle those settings. This is something that you can do on a periodic basis or all at once. But it's good to keep checking back. I'm primarily referring to the settings for your social networks, e-mail, and video-game consoles. Go to the settings menu and ensure that you've checked the right boxes to protect your privacy, keep spam or reminders to a minimum, and lock away whatever you don't want the kids to see or play. Be the settings police. No one else is going to do it for you, and it will give you renewed peace of mind.

iFitness (iPhone): There are countless apps to craft your workout, but one of the better-rated ones is iFitness. It costs $1.99 and lists dozens of exercises targeted to specific parts of your body, a food tracker that breaks down nutritional content, and a way to customize your workout by choosing a part of your body to focus on.

traineo (Web): There are dozens of strategies out there to help you structure your weight-loss program. One of the more science based is at the Web site traineo.com. The first thing you'll need is a scale to measure your weight daily. For some people that's a daunting number to stare at every day, but the app is designed to track your fatty ups and downs over time and suggest the right calorie count. Once you've entered your weight each day, the software illustrates your advancement on a line graph based on your food choices and even helps smooth out concerns over day-to-day fluctuations in weight (gaining a pound or two here and there doesn't mean you've ballooned into a whale but may be tied to a number of different variables). It'll even predict your future weight given your behavior, and of course the goal is to enter a target weight/date for the overarching project. To make it all a little more interactive, the traineo community offers tips and tricks for an exercise regimen and shares various weight-loss plan results (Paleo vs. South Beach). It's quick, easy, and visual. I mean the app, not the weight loss. Sometimes that's slow, tough, and hard to see. But with a personal trainer and a mini chef in your pocket you may be more apt to stick with it.

Dinner Spinner, Laundry Pal, Grocery iQ (iPhone, iPod, iPad, Android): There are a variety of programs that will help you better manage day-to-day chores, too. Dinner Spinner lets you input whatever ingredients you have on hand (or a target nutritional value) and puts together a range of possible dishes. Laundry Pal helps decode those cryptic illustrations on clothing tags, and Grocery iQ lets you share your grocery list with others (so there's no doubling up), scan bar codes (using your smart phone camera) to find the best deal, and even have coupons sent directly to your loyalty card.

CogniFit (Web): CogniFit is a Web site that tailors a cognitive "training" program to your schedule and your needs. Through a brief introduction and test, the site measures your responses to a variety of simple challenges involving memory, shape matching, and puzzle solving. It begins with a baseline of your cognitive abilities, and then a few times a week (for about twenty minutes per day) you run through a series of exercises meant to improve your mental muscles. There's even one to help seniors refresh their driving skills. A monthly subscription costs $19.95, or one year goes for $179.95. It has a number of mental-health partners and touts Olympian Bruce Jenner among its supporters. It's not the cheapest option out there, but spending some money might also make you stick with it.

Fooducate (iPhone)/FatSecret Calorie Counter (Android): Reading the back label of any food product to see what's really inside is a no-brainer. But deciphering the names of those ingredients and how they might affect your body is a whole other challenge. That's where Fooducate can, well, educate you about the food you eat. After downloading the free app, you can use the camera on your iPhone to scan bar codes and get an instant rundown of bad ingredients and important information. It also ranks foods on a scale of "A" to "F" and suggests healthier alternatives. For Android phone users, FatSecret Calorie Counter keeps track of caloric intake and also uses the camera to scan bar codes for nutritional content information.

Console Cardio

According to a Pew survey from 2008, more than half of U.S. adults play some kind of video games (55 percent of men and 50 percent of women). On the youth side, a staggering 97 percent of teens play some kind of video game. Do the math, and that amounts to most Americans at least having a video-game console (such as an Xbox 360, PlayStation 3, or Nintendo Wii) in the home. In addition, every video-game console on the market has now tapped into motion-control technology—Nintendo got rolling first with the Wii; Sony has followed with its Move controllers; and Microsoft offers a similar interaction with its Kinect, except *you* are the controller. (Wii uses a sensor bar to detect where the Wii controllers are moving; PlayStation 3 uses a camera, which it claims is more accurate and better able to "see" the movement of the controllers; and Kinect goes a step further, using a 3-D camera and other sensors that "see" where your body is—no controller required.)

And a growing number of titles target adults (particularly women) with workouts like yoga, dancing, and even running. Some games, like Sony's Sports Champions or the Your Shape game for Kinect, offer obvious ways to get your heart rate up, like playing table tennis. But there are also plenty of games that get you moving without forcing you to exercise. Easily one of the most popular is Dance Dance Revolution, or "DDR," as it's commonly known. Another is Dance Central for the Xbox Kinect. If you want to take it one step further, devices like the Game-Runner system allow you to jog (or walk) through a computer-generated 3-D world or online virtual world. It takes up more space than your average video-game console and might feel a little foreign,

TechFact

A study from the *Archives of Pediatrics and Adolescent Medicine* found that active video games (AVGs), such as the Wii Fit, do increase physical activity in children and adolescents. The study found that with AVGs, children increased their energy expenditure by 222 percent and increased their heart rate by 64 percent.

but it's certainly on the higher end of exercise interaction.

Here's the bottom line: there are a growing number of ways to use technology that's already in your home to add at least a modicum of a workout to your routine. There's nothing stopping you from doing it *with* the kids, too. Granted, it can look a tad silly. And there's no guarantee that it'll help you drop all the necessary pounds and get back to your "fighting weight." But if you have any inclination or curiosity at all, it's worth the attempt. The games offer ingenious ways to keep you coming back (e.g., tracking your progress with a profile, showing calories burned). Worst-case scenario: your kids might

Exercise Day 11

Flex those toes. It's not exactly scientific, but it works. I first saw it while watching *Die Hard*. Bruce Willis's character sits with bare feet on the carpet and scrunches up his toes and then releases them as a way to combat jet lag. Try it. Do it for about five to seven minutes in the morning and then again in the evening. It takes your mind off the stresses of the day and actually feels pretty good.

look at you in a whole different way (like you're crazy—just kidding). Video games are here to stay, and instead of always railing against them, it could be worth turning the tables and finding a beneficial place for them in your home.

The Alarming Clock

Because cell phones are extremely accurate at keeping time, they are very reliable as alarm clocks. That, coupled with the ability to use a fun ringtone for a wake-up sound or choose a favorite song or download an alarm app, makes it even more attractive to use smart phones this way. The problem is this: we end up with our smart phones and cell phones right next to us in bed every night and every morning, the very place and time at which we're meant to get some rest. That's counterproductive. It's a constant temptation. So while the device is charging its batteries, it's preventing you from fully charging yours.

Take Action: From now on, plug your phone into an outlet in the kitchen. Buy a cheap alarm clock. You can get a decent one for under fifteen dollars. It will accomplish the same goal of rousing your sleepy head from bed, and you can rest knowing that during the evening hours you will not be inclined to surf the Web or check e-mail or send texts. (Plus you won't come to hate your bed as yet another area invaded by technology.) It will also change the way you view your device—in other words, you won't see it as this annoying person next to your bed screaming, "WAKE UP AND SPEAK TO ME RIGHT NOW!!!" That's really what you're doing by placing your phone there. You're giving it permission to make you frazzled and furious. Once you reply to a single e-mail and then hear back, it's all over: your e-day has started. (At the very least, if

TechFact

During the three months ending in July 2010, 31.4 percent of mobile users aged thirteen and up downloaded apps. In the previous three-month period, 29.8 percent had done so.

you must have your smart phone near your bed, then turn off the wireless and cellular signal so it's being used purely as an alarm clock.)

App-ed Out?

Apps, apps, apps. Sick of the apps? If 2009 was the year that everyone seemed to adopt a smart phone, then 2010 became the year that everyone wanted to populate said smart phone with tiny programs or applications called "apps." Nearly every smart phone has some kind of app store, though the largest is Apple's iTunes. As of late 2010, there were more than 250,000 apps available (and counting) in the iTunes app store alone—an unknown number of those capable of recreating the sound of flatulence.

That said, as I've pointed out, there are many apps that make life better or more manageable and will even help you with your Digital Diet. Right now I want to focus on the sheer number of apps and how we consume them. It can be overwhelming, to say the least. And there are lots of crap apps. But there are plenty of apps that serve a purpose beyond just health (check Wi-Fi strength, buy movie tickets, get subway directions, locate the nearest bathroom), and I'm suggesting you check out ones that help you. But it's important to organize and maintain your app collection in a beneficial manner, because for every useful app there are scores of dumb ones out there. The average app user gets bored with an app in seven to ten days. Of course, that's great news for Apple ("Oh, what's one more? It's only ninety-nine cents"), but it means that we're all becoming a tad app addicted.

Consider this: the typical smart phone allows you to swipe across various home screens—I'd recommend keeping your apps to two pages. That usually amounts to a dozen or so apps. Lots of room to play with some silly apps and test out one or two that might work for you. But I see people who scroll through pages and pages of apps on their smart phone and wonder how they keep track. Why so many? Surely there isn't a real need for all of them. Try them out, then incorporate them if they make sense or delete them if they don't. No one is being a killjoy—get the Angry Birds or Fruit Ninja apps along with the handy ones. Just swap out the ones you're not using for the ones that have a place in your life. It's a bit like buying new socks and throwing out the old ones with holes in them. If you don't, your drawer just gets cluttered and you wonder why on earth you can't throw them out. One pair of socks probably costs as much as some apps. So sock it to your smart phone and keep a regular flow of apps. (Note: you can also use a smart phone just fine without buying or using any apps at all.) So use some of the apps I mentioned if they "app-eal" to you, and cycle them through on a regular basis.

I also encourage you to explore other apps and programs that might stimulate your brain and give you a chance to improve your (virtual) IQ. Think about what works best for you and your family. Use what works. There's no harm in trying various programs (so long as you don't overdo it with the apps), and in the next chapters we'll review even more ways to reconnect. Surge ahead!

8

Upbeat While Downloading

Days 12–15

"If it keeps up, man will atrophy all his limbs but the push-button finger."

—**Frank Lloyd Wright**

This is more of the good stuff. In this section, I will encourage you to explore new and emerging technologies or Web sites that benefit your life, and I'd like you to delve into at least one of these per day. It might mean reading about a new product, or it might mean actually purchasing something. The goal is to start making technol-

Exercise Day 12

Before we get into the "stuff," let's start with an exercise that doesn't require any money and could pay you back in unseen ways: a gratitude section in your journal. This is a fairly straightforward exercise and not unique to the Digital Diet approach. But it's worthwhile nonetheless. Throughout the course of the days and weeks, before you go to bed, write down the top two or three people or events that you are most thankful for. It doesn't have to be much. And of course it can be private. The birth of your children. A snuggle with your dog. Feeling the sun on your face. You can even tear out the page from your journal, fold up the piece of paper, and put it in your wallet or purse. That's all. Just simple words to remember and inspire.

ogy work for you. And have some fun doing it! But remember to keep your e-day close to a maximum of ninety minutes (again, outside of any essential work-related stuff). Think about when you begin your day plugging in and when you officially unplug.

Give yourself borders and boundaries. I'll expand on that more later. For now, continue the journey.

Cancel the Noise

Here are a few digital ways to help you focus and be productive. This technology may just help you get *more* done.

Noise-canceling headphones: Noise-canceling headphones are a gift from the heavens that are individually kissed by a series of angels. Hyperbole for a reason. Invest in a pair of these candies for your ears. Not only will you shut out the irritating and distracting sounds around you (most wonderful while at work or, of course, on an airplane), but you will also likely begin to funnel your attention better on the task in front of you. They're like blinders (for your ears) keeping your thoroughbred performance on track. Do not hesitate; do not pass "Go"; spend the two-hundred-plus dollars on noise-canceling headphones and incorporate them into your Digital Diet arsenal. At the very least, put them on your wish list and see if someone comes through. They are well worth the money. (Just don't make them an excuse to be antisocial.)

ChatterBlocker: For less money, or in combination with noise-canceling headphones, there is a program called ChatterBlocker that may be a sanity saver for anyone who works in a cubicle environment. You choose from a series of sound combinations (e.g., nature and music, voices and music) or just single sounds (e.g., voices, nature) that are meant to dull any surrounding noise to a minimal drone. The music selections aren't all that memorable, but that's the point—they're meant to be unobtrusive and soothing. The purpose is to make intelligible sound unintelligible to eliminate distraction. One of their selling points is that they allow you to "hear yourself think." Some of the combinations are a bit much, but generally they have a calming effect. The full version costs $19.95, but you can try out a demo version for free.

tawkon (smart phones): I should preface this section by saying I'm not entirely convinced one way or the other that cell-phone radiation is dangerous. The studies are almost evenly divided between concern and disregard (of course moderation is still key). However, it's no secret that cell phones do emit teeny tiny bits of radiation, and there may be good reason to learn to limit and alter our intake over time. So as part of the Digital Diet, you might want to consider an app like tawkon, which was created by an Israeli company. It claims to be the first app embedded *in* your phone that can detect the radiation levels around it. It's available for iPhone, BlackBerry, Android, and Nokia's Symbian operating systems among others.

The idea of tawkon is that the phone will signal you when you've reached a high intake of radiation. It will suggest perhaps turning the phone from horizontal to vertical, moving your hand away from the antenna on the bottom (to reduce the radiation coming into you), or using a speakerphone or earpiece. Tawkon can also tap into the phone's GPS and guide the user to an area with less radiation nearby (a "green zone"). It's not without merit, given the never-ending debate about the subject, and with San Francisco having recently enacted a law forcing cell-phone makers to label boxes with radiation output, it's sure to be a hot topic (no pun intended) in years to come. For now you can always look up your cell-phone radiation on the FCC Web site and, as part of your Digital Diet, spend less time blabbing away and make those cell-phone calls count.

ValleyZen (Web): Technology should inspire our lives, not interrupt them. And every attempt should be made to give our devices and online interactions a sense of energized calm. If that mantra sounds rather Zen-like, that's because it is. One of the great resources online for adhering to that empowering position is ValleyZen.com. Through a series of articles, videos, and blog posts, the site offers a refreshing approach to simplicity and efficiency by challenging people to rethink their dependence on technology. It's about turning the slave into the master by shaking up the routine. For example, here are the site's seven principles of Zen aesthetics, with my interpretations of their technological applications in parentheses:

++ Fukinsei: asymmetry or imbalance
    *(Don't get caught up in checking every
    e-mail all the time.)*

++ Kanso: simplicity or elimination of
    clutter
    *(Keep your favorite sites to a minimum,
    close down old accounts, and avoid carry-
    ing too many devices.)*

++ Koko: austerity or bare essentials
    *(Streamline your devices, services, and even
    contact list.)*

++ Shizen: naturalness or unforced creativity
    *(Allow your mind to wander away from the
    gadgets.)*

++ Yugen: profundity or suggestion, rather than revelation
(Embrace the moment and live in the present without seeking attention through your devices.)

++ Datsuzoku: freedom from habit or formula
(Regular log-ins can be fine, but shake it up once in a while—feel in control.)

++ Seijaku: tranquility or energized calm
(Take those walks, take deep breaths, and use your other senses.)

One of the site's cofounders, Drue Kataoka, is one of the most magnetic people you'll ever meet. She exudes calm in her relationship with technology, yet she wields it in a powerful way, having developed a number of start-up companies (her latest is PassportStyle.com). To me it's very similar to the way a samurai would view his sword; there is respect without getting caught up in the power. See your devices as that sword.

Lifetick (iPhone and Android): Lists, lists, lists. I seem to make a new list every day and sometimes a list to remind me to make more lists. They're like meetings: innately maddening yet admittedly nec-

Exercise Day 13

One of my favorite pieces of advice from Kataoka is to use the power of subtraction. We often get too caught up in adding more information to a presentation or throwing more graphics on a Web site or adding more bookmarks to our browser. Technology makes it easy to load up with more and more services and gadgets and e-stuff. For a change, take a day and minimize your digital landscape. Remove a bookmark that you don't use, or strip away some of your old e-mails or contacts. Shed some of the noise that you don't need. Your power will lie not only in the end result of feeling less bogged down but also in the decision-making process of eliminating certain aspects of your technology—the choosing and the sorting.

essary. Along comes a clever little app that might help your desire to keep track of the lists in your life and see the results along the way. Lifetick's goal is to help you reach your goals, such as studying for an exam or training for a triathlon or finishing the renovations on your house. First you establish your core values, like career, family, and health. Then you create a list of tasks. For example, for home renovations the task list might include visiting the showroom, deciding on various contractors, choosing appliances, etc. The software then prompts you at various times if you determine that you need e-mail reminders and creates pie charts and bar graphs to map your progress. The app itself is free, and for an additional twenty dollars per month you can use it with a group of employees or colleagues to monitor the path toward a shared goal. It's basic but beneficial and clearly a solid example of "positive computing."

TechFact

A study from 2009 suggests that the same neurons that process the primitive physical rewards of food and water also signal the more abstract mental rewards of receiving information. Put another way: discovering the answer to an elusive question can potentially trigger the same response in your cranium as taking a sip of a fine wine.

Springpad (iPhone, iPad, Web, Android):
Springpad is like a calendar/organizer on steroids.
It's a free program that can be downloaded onto
your smart phone and your laptop (both offer a
similar interface). You can jot down notes, keep
track of chores, and save recipes or anything else
you come across while surfing the Web. Those saved
items can then be categorized and linked together,
which makes them easier to search and browse,
whether you're at home or on the go. For example,
if you like a particular type of wine you taste while
at a friend's place for dinner, you can quickly write
down the name, save any information it finds online
during a quick search, and move on. That's what I
like about it—Springpad is designed to get you in
and out of the digital space in short order. Think
of it as your own personal assistant (without the
attitude).

Digsby (Web): If you simply can't live without
all your social networks and instant message programs and e-mail alerts, then Digsby might be the
tool for you. It's a free piece of software that lives
on your desktop. The idea is that it pulls all your
sites together in one place. You can include several
e-mail, social-network, and messaging programs
by adding each one (putting in your passwords

and logging on). The program is customizable, so you can include whichever services you want and, say, give your buddies easier-to-remember aliases (like "Laura" instead of her login name "twilight _fan_8903"). The news feed can be tweaked, too, and I encourage you to think about what you need versus what's available. Putting these services in one place should at least save you time and brain-

Exercise Day 14

Review your smart-phone plan. Every month we get a bill from our wireless carrier and often just ignore the options to change it or tailor it for our lifestyle. Go through your plan, line by line, and see what can be adjusted based on your needs and usage. For example, having an unlimited option can be great in terms of saving money, but remember that the temptation to send endless texts could be harmful too, in terms of doing that in lieu of a conversation. Consider the bottom line from a financial perspective as well as a social one. And don't be afraid to gather the whole family around to discuss it.

power over shifting back and forth among all of them. But don't let Digsby take over. Let it come to you, and remember to log out when you feel overwhelmed by it.

fidipidi (**Web**): This is a pretty clever idea that merges new-age with old-school. Once you go to the site, you'll need to log on to your Facebook page and add fidipidi as an app. Keep in mind that that means giving the app some amount of access to your personal data, and I don't usually recommend that, so there is a worthwhile trade-off here. Basically, you can upload any photo to Facebook and design your own paper card to be mailed (yes, snail mailing still exists). The key with this program is to send cards to the people who really matter. If you have 756 friends, well, it would be (a) impractical and (b) a bit silly/expensive to try to send a fidipidi card to all of them. Identify the people who you know would get a delightful jolt from seeing a real card in the mail, and go ahead and send it. Now, if only they included a camera so you could see your friend's reaction when they open it.

ThankThankNotes (**Web**): Handwritten thank-you cards are a tall order even for the most dedicated Miss Manners among us (plus, your handwriting might not be what it used to be). But what if someone wrote the notes for you? That's the promise of ThankThankNotes.com, a Web site that lets you type a message (up to seventy-five words) and then turn it into a series of handwritten cards. Each card costs three dollars and can be customized based on the occasion. You can even specify whether the handwriting looks like it's from a male or a female (see the Web site's examples), and the company is considering adding options for handwriting that's either barely legible or elegant. You can import contact information from Outlook and the company will stuff, seal, and send the cards. Should it replace all your personal correspondence? Of course not. But it can be a fun alternative to e-mail and should at least make the recipient smile. (Plus, sending carrier pigeons is just too messy.)

Attack Spam

Speaking of e-mail, you might've thought that by now spam would be a thing of the past, a side effect of the rapid growth of the Internet that disappeared as we all wised up. Not so much. It's still out there, but you don't have to be overwhelmed by it. The basics still apply—don't open strange e-mails or click on links from banks or other financial institutions in unsolicited messages. And don't sign up for any online service unless you're prepared to get hit with plenty of unwanted e-mails. Spam thrives because some people out there are actually clicking on this stuff. Otherwise they'd pack up and go home. One handy tool that should minimize some of the junk: when asked by a site to provide a working e-mail address (maybe to sign up for a service), try Mailinator .com. Simply make up any e-mail address you can imagine (e.g., goofballfrenchfries@mailinator.com) and use that to sign up for the service. The confirmation e-mail will go to goofballfrenchfries@ mailinator.com, and by going to Mailinator.com you can log in to your account using that e-mail name and click on the link to verify it as a real e-mail account. That account is then cleared out within a day or two. It's like a temporary dumping ground for any e-mails you don't really need for very long. Another such site is myTrashMail.com.

Or you could beef up your existing e-mail using a program from the likes of Symantec (Brightmail), Firetrust (MailWasher), or SPAMfighter. The cost varies from free for the temporary e-mail addresses to upwards of twenty-five dollars for the software. These days, Web-based e-mail programs like Gmail and Yahoo! are doing a much better job of filtering spam, but you can also set manual filters based on keywords like "lottery" or "hair loss" or "enlargement." Deleting spam can be time-consuming at the very least, and falling victim to spam scams like "phishing" (which tries to steal your identity through fake financial Web sites) can be downright crippling. Vigilance remains your best option—until all those spammers get a conscience.

Yeah, right.

To Skype or Not to Skype

We can agree that Skype and other webcam/phone services can be a fantastic part of staying in touch over long distances. But they come with a new set of problems. Including Skype in your Digital Diet is worthwhile, but it must be done with a series of caveats. Skype with video is not like talking on the phone. Yes, you can see the person, which means you might need to brush your hair or put on some clothes. But with a cell-phone call you can dial someone up and ask if you're interrupting them. Don't expect the same with Skype. People will readily ignore a request to chat on Skype if they

Exercise Day 15

Attack the unread messages. By that I mean I want you to get those untidy e-mails in order. If this exercise takes more than your allotted time for being online (remember the ninety-minutes guideline), then stretch it out over a few days. Create some folders with specific headings (e.g., "immediate," "later," "rainy day") to help prioritize your messages. And use that delete key with reckless abandon. Fashion experts will

don't feel up to it or don't want to "perform" in front of the camera. To a lesser degree, the same goes for instant messaging. Both technologies present a list of people who might be online. That doesn't mean they're ready and willing to talk to you. And the fact that Skype is also free means you might tend to linger rather than be efficient. Of course, have those moments of showcasing the grandchild, give a tour of the new apartment thanks to a wireless connection and a laptop, and enjoy the visual connection of seeing people's facial reactions. All often say if you haven't worn something for an entire year, then you probably won't wear it again and don't need it. A similar rule can be applied to e-mail. Web-based programs allow us to keep thousands of messages and make it easy to search them. And if you prefer that way of maintaining your contacts and data, then it's fine to keep them. But seek to get that unread number down to zero.

good things. But don't let Skype invade your life too much, and ensure that you keep limits when necessary. Keep the connections meaningful and worthwhile.

"Ten and Two"

Texting while driving has almost become a national epidemic. Certainly there are too many related injuries and deaths, and they're totally avoidable. I've interviewed the father of a young boy who was killed by a woman texting while driving. She plowed into the side of the family's SUV while running a red light. Was she mindlessly texting a friend about her date last night? No, she was texting with her church. So the intent and the motivation and the excuses don't matter—just put the device down and drive. If the temptation is still too great, there are programs that can force you to quit. They can also be great for teenagers. For example, take the NOTXT n' Drive app for the BlackBerry. Using GPS, it runs in the background and shuts off texting while the car (device) is moving faster than ten miles per hour (which is much faster than most people walk). With another app called iZUP (for Android and BlackBerry), outgoing e-mails, texts, and calls are blocked entirely (calling 911 is still possible). Passengers can override it with a password-protected feature. It costs $2.95 per month. And if driving too fast is an issue, then you can always try Slow Down (for iPhone, iPad, and iPod). Using GPS, it detects your speed, and if you exceed a preset speed limit your music will slow down until you do. Go more than ten miles per hour over, and it'll stop entirely. Obviously, the best approach to safe driving is staying focused on the road and minimizing distractions. But for some people a little high-tech help can go a long way. You know who you are.

You're Getting Sleepy . . .

One of the most welcome categories of inventions in the past hundred years would have to be gadgets that help you sleep. Who among us couldn't use a better path to more zzzzzz's? You definitely don't need all of these devices, but they're at least worth considering.

Clocky: For thirty dollars, Clocky is a durable little alarm clock with rubber wheels attached to its sides. When it's time for wakey wakey, Clocky takes a jumpy jumpy off your night table. No more snooze bar, and definitely no more using your smart phone to wake you up. No doubt it's annoying as it crashes around the room, but it takes your devices out of the equation and probably guarantees getting your butt out of bed.

Philips Wake-Up Light: There are a few different companies that make similar "sunrise emulators" (BioBrite, Northern Light Technologies), but the idea is the same: a slow introduction to light and sound (rather than "BAAANNNHHH BAAANNNHHH

BAAANNNHHH") will let the pixie dust of the night disappear in a more soothing manner. The prices hover around $125.

Sleeptracker PRO watch: This one sounds a bit far-fetched, and the reviews of it on sites like Amazon.com are mixed, but overall the concept appears to work. Basically, the watch uses internal sensors to gauge when it's best to wake you based on your sleep cycle. You can also look back at your night's sleep and see if it might've been restless or restful. Not a cheap investment at $175, so maybe sleep on it first.

An Ongoing Quest

There are always new technologies and apps and doodads coming to the market that are aimed at improving your life. Others help restrain certain aspects of your life—they might be called "detech-ing" apps or "outsourcing self-control." In the last couple of chapters I've touched on only a handful of them that I think could work with your Digital Diet. In fact, this part of the diet will ultimately be organic in nature and evolve over time through various tips that people share online. Don't be afraid to check out other technologies that might work for you—but don't feel compelled to add them to your diet unless they work. Maintain that focus and that simplicity. The choices are yours. You can do it!

9

This Time
It's Personal

Days 16–18

*"Technology . . . is a queer thing. It brings
you great gifts with one hand, and it stabs
you in the back with the other."*

—C. P. Snow, scientist and novelist, 1971

For the next few days, you will be encouraged to rekindle face-to-face relationships with friends and family members. Our real social network. The goal is to reconnect with people with whom you've lost touch and to go about repairing those ties. It won't be easy. Serving as an example, I will delve into some of my struggles on this front, as until recently I had lost touch with many folks in my life, including my sister. We'll also explore the impact the psychological professionals claim digital communication has on our relationships and our privacy. The goal of this period of the Digital Diet is to set up a date and follow through in person. It can be as simple as a coffee-shop meeting or as elaborate as a family vacation.

Exercise Day 16

Reading facial expressions has become something of a lost art, as we spend so much time engrossed in the glow of our mobile device. Take the time to really observe people as you go through your day—the server at the coffee shop, the tollbooth worker, your neighbor. Make an effort to look them in the eye when you interact with them, and read their expressions. You'll be amazed by how many more cues you'll pick up and how deeply you'll sense the nuance of a particular comment.

No Fences Make
for a Lot of Neighbors

So why bother with privacy? That's the argument that Facebook founder Mark Zuckerberg made in January 2010 when he told a group of reporters and analysts that, in essence, the age of privacy is over. Zuckerberg said that Internet users have become comfortable sharing plenty of information "more openly and with more people" than ever before, referring to it as the new "social norm." When you read that, are you (a) nodding your head in agreement, (b) shocked and appalled, (c) wondering where the time went, or (d) all of the above?

The idea that being wired weakens our hold on privacy is not new. Back in 1999 Sun cofounder Scott McNealy was famously quoted saying: "You have zero privacy anyway. Get over it." Well, perhaps in many ways we have "gotten over it" and relaxed our barriers on personal information. We share photos, we post phone numbers, we voice opinions. And on the surface there seem to be very few drawbacks, if any. What's the big deal if we expose more of our lives? We're sharing that stuff with people and learning more about them along the way. It seems the exception when someone's personal identity is stolen or there's an overzealous person following your every move or you get hit with an unsolicited message or request.

Ask Yourself: Would you literally stand in front of your colleagues and friends and family and yell everything you post online? The answer is almost universally "no." Yet I doubt many people run that test before posting a status update or sending a tweet.

If a twenty-first-century existence means swimming in a sea of data every day, who needs a life preserver? You do. Aside from your friends (both real and virtual) who follow your online exploits, there are hundreds of marketers and companies snatching up every shred of your Internet habits, choices, and blunders. Hidden within the navel-gazing and drunken party photos and grandstanding are ways for companies to target you or offer discounts or spam you with e-mail. They search for keywords and trends. They devour product references or the number of times you "like" something. Those tidbits about you can be intensely personal (not to mention embarrassing: "sooooooo drink rghtt now i cn barelyy cee"). You may have already blocked out the obvious interlopers by switching your privacy settings from "Everyone" to "Friends Only," but how do you respond when you receive friend requests from work colleagues or little-known family members? The temptation to share with new people or see what their lives are like is pretty powerful. Our tendency to sacrifice online privacy has coincided with sacrificing the quality of real-world interactions. We're letting the desire for recognition replace the desire for connection.

I'm not sure how many of you have come close to deleting or deactivating your social networks, but I want to be clear that I'm not trying to convince people that social networks are all bad. Or that they have the same effect on everybody. But I do think their rapid rise in popularity and acceptance has reached a tipping point: many of us are starting to realize that expanding our online social lives can cause our offline networks to deteriorate.

One of the interesting sidebars to my experiment with eliminating social networks in my life occurred on January 5, 2010, which is my birthday. On my birthday in 2008 and 2009, my Facebook wall was decorated with all sorts of well-wishes and greetings and "gifts." It was a bit overwhelming, actually, but of course it was nice that people felt compelled to post something. But in 2010 I only heard from the people in my life who knew how to reach me offline (and knew the date of my birthday—no Facebook reminder). Of course, there's nothing wrong with reminders, but when it comes to celebrations it seems as though online shout-outs and text messages have replaced the infinitely more satisfying birthday card or phone call.

Which would you prefer? Consider whether fifty

Exercise Day 17

Set your phone to give no vibration or audio alerts for e-mails or texts. Even when we don't pick it up, we're all tempted to glance at a device that lights up or vibrates. It's an interruption and clearly rude. Try to keep using these no-alert settings after your Digital Diet is complete. Having your smart phone alert you of phone calls is fine, but given the frequency of other types of communication, sometimes a phone alert goes off once a minute. Don't let your device be a chirping nag in your pocket. Check it when you choose to and on your own time.

wall posts can replace one actual birthday card. Auntie Smelly's card in the mail can still make us pause and smile. Remember that. If you enjoy receiving it, then someone else will, too.

Getting Friendly

Being off social networks also got me thinking about what defines a "friend." In addition to the great people I've met in recent years, I've been lucky to have the same close friends since high school back in Canada. We were dorky kids back then, and now we're dorky adults. These are some smart, caring, and wonderful people whom I treasure. I would trust them with my life. But we're now scattered to the four corners of the earth, and it isn't easy to see one another in person.

Most of them are on Facebook, but I wouldn't consider them overly active users. And yet a couple of years ago I realized that I'd drifted away from the more meaningful means of distance communication (e.g., phone calls, Skype, e-mail, etc.) and relied too heavily on just reading status updates or checking out photos. Sure, it's one way to stay in touch, but it's awfully shallow. Increasingly, I felt out of the

TechFact

According to a Yahoo! Research study published in the *Journal of Personality and Social Psychology*, users of social networks "do not seem to base their perceptions of their friends' views on what they talk about, but rather on some combination of their own opinions (projection) and of what they assume about their friends (stereotyping)."

loop. But I kept "broadcasting" what I was doing and thinking, "Oh well, this is how the world interacts today," with a curious but passive level of interest. But you don't have to accept that, and I'll show you how not to.

Your Turn?

In mid-February 2010, not long after I lost my job, I got a call rather late at night. Now, I hate to admit this, but prior to my social-networking experiment and the Digital Diet, I might've ignored a call at that hour and retreated into my shell. I selfishly wanted communication on my terms. But my sister and I had recently talked about my path to better communication, and I answered her call. Plus, I missed her a lot. She sounded shaky and anxious. I knew she might be exhausted from her final year of nursing studies, but the tension in her voice seemed like more than just homework woes. I told her I was in the process of editing my reel (the TV version of a résumé), and she said maybe it'd be best to talk another time. But I insisted that she tell me what was on her mind. (I was secretly hoping that it was that her boyfriend had proposed, although that didn't jibe with her tone.) Then she said it point blank: a brain tumor had been discovered during a routine MRI. I barely heard her say "benign," and I clung to that word for dear life.

We talked a bit more, we cried some, and I made plans to head to Toronto, where she lives. I was there three days later. Had I not spent the preceding several weeks working to reestablish our one-on-one communication, it's possible my sister would not have decided to call me right away. I wasn't being the best brother when it came to staying in touch. And a brain tumor isn't usually the kind of thing you announce as a status update. Ultimately, my Digital Diet has brought me so much closer to my sister in her time of need, and I can't imagine how it used to be. I never want to go back. (She's doing okay, relatively speaking. The doctors don't want to operate yet for fear of what the surgery could do. For now they're monitoring it and taking a wait-and-see approach.)

Now that I've outlined in some detail how I made my personal journey away from social networks and closer to friends and family, I want to offer you the tools to do the same. Tackling your dependency on social networks is a sizable part of the Digital Diet. In the end, you may decide to either keep your presence on them but scale back how much you use them or eliminate them altogether. Keep in mind that there are ways to temporarily remove yourself from social networks with the option of returning later, so don't feel that it's all or nothing. For example, you can deactivate your Facebook profile so it doesn't show up on the Facebook site, but the information you've already posted will remain in the company's servers and could still show up in Google search results or elsewhere. Deactivating your profile (whether it's Facebook or Twitter or MySpace) is a way to minimize your temptation and perhaps test the limits of how and why you use it. If you wish to delete your profile entirely, that's (mostly) permanent and can be a major step for some people. Before considering either deactivation or deletion, let's go over some settings changes that could at least make your social-network life more tolerable.

Take Action: In Facebook, under the "Account" section, click on "Privacy Settings." Unless you want a raft of strangers to have your personal details, ensure that "friends only" can view your shared information, from status updates to photos. Next, click on "Account Settings" under "Account." First stop—click on Facebook Ads and activate the setting to show your information to "No one." No point making life that easy for marketers. Next, under "Notifications," reduce (by unchecking the boxes) the number of notifications you get via e-mail or text when someone makes a change to their page or adds you as a friend or comments on a photo that you commented on. Keeping those notifications to a dull roar will curb your temptation to log in all the time and make you feel less harangued by your friends.

If you want to deactivate your profile, it's a little harder to do. Under "Account," click on "Account Settings," then scroll down to the bottom and click "Deactivate Account." You'll be faced with photos of friends and the words "So-and-so will miss you." If you follow through with deactivation, then your profile will not be accessible to users but the information will remain on Facebook's servers and you can easily reactivate your profile with any activity on the site (e.g., logging on again). To delete it entirely, the best approach is to click on the tiny "Help" link in the lower-right corner of the screen and then click on the "Top Question" link on the upper-right that reads "How Do I Permanently Delete My Account?" Scroll down and submit your request to have it deleted, and ultimately your account and all the information you shared will be gone. Facebook warns that this information will be unrecoverable, though there is some debate as to whether it will actually be purged from Facebook's servers. But if you really want to be sure your account is dead and buried, read on.

Web 2.0 Suicide Machine

I like to refer to the guy behind this project as the Jack Kevorkian of social networks. Now, I don't necessarily advocate killing yourself (virtually or otherwise), but if your Digital Diet requires a complete removal of your social network presence, then Web 2.0 Suicide Machine might be for you. Based in the Netherlands, it was started as an art project by Gordan Savicic during a New Year's Eve celebration in 2008 where people decided to quit their social networks. Here's the gist: You hand over your passwords and log-in information for all of your social networks. Once you reach the top of the company's long waiting list, the program will systematically remove all traces of your profile and postings and all other traces of your online life (or at least bury any search results in, say, Google, at the very bottom). It's a time-consuming process, and you can actually

Exercise Day 18

Send at least five e-mails during your allotted time to someone you love. They don't have to be too long, but make them personal. No group messages, and nothing dismissive or throwaway. Take the time to craft a worthwhile message. E-mail can be overwhelming, and there will be days when you want to blow up your in-box. But today keep it intimate and heartfelt.

TechFact

In a Duke University study, according to *Time* magazine, researchers found that from 1985 to 2004, the percentage of people who said there was no one with whom they discussed important matters tripled, to 25 percent; the same study found that overall, Americans had one-third fewer friends and confidants than they did two decades ago.

watch some of it happen in real time on your computer. People have even posted their virtual demises as YouTube videos. Keep in mind that it's irreversible (much like death itself) and isn't for the faint of heart. But Web 2.0 Suicide Machine reflects an interesting trend in today's society, as we sometimes feel the need to "kill" our virtual selves to regain better control over our real ones.

Positive Vibes

In the course of assembling this Digital Diet, I spoke to dozens of experts in the fields of technology, psychology, and health. One of the most interesting movements that seem to touch on all three areas is "positive computing." It's a growing movement, and it encompasses a broad range of ideals. For example, positive computing would like to see more smart-phone apps that offer people reinforcement throughout their day, like an app that remembers your favorite photos and cycles through them when you click on it. Or a program for your laptop or computer that assembles your most positive and glowing e-mails—so that you can read them over, à la Al Franken's character Stuart Smalley from *Saturday Night Live* ("Goshdarnit people like me"), before going into that stressful meeting or presentation. Or a program that collects upbeat references to your coworkers ("Appreciate it, Sally!") to read when the rigors of working together become too much. The people behind positive computing are also working with military service people to give them better ways to stay in touch and find distractions while on duty as well as deal with post-traumatic stress disorder when they return home.

Linda Stone, a former executive at both Apple and Microsoft, is one of the driving forces behind the positive-computing movement. Stone is one of those people who manage to compartmentalize their use of technology in the most wonderful fashion. While we had lunch at a busy café, she was quick to point out that although her smart phone was on the table, she would not be checking it unless the incoming message related to her next appointment or was an emergency. (That's a great tip—acknowledge the device on the table; don't just dump it there like a tech turd.) Stone likes to reinforce the idea of "sensing and feeling" instead of "acting and doing." I know that sounds a little hippie-ish, and I hope Linda isn't offended when I say that I sense some of that sixties-era spirit within her. But my take is that technology tends to numb our senses. It's like a suit of armor that protects us from an unseen enemy—yet the irony is that we end up becoming our own worst enemy. Pushing buttons and receiving information and reading short blurbs isn't living.

So what do I mean by that? We've all seen those calendars or screen savers or desktop wallpapers with glorious images of a sandy beach. The water is magical and turquoise and tranquil. There are no statistics on how many people have downloaded such material over the years, but I suspect it's very high. They're an escape hatch. A portal. A place to which we wish we could teleport. I also suspect that the vast majority within that group doesn't ever visit that place. It remains elusive and tantalizing and, frankly, tormenting. Well, that's letting technology get the best of you without actually getting off your ass and doing something about it. Seriously. No one is holding a gun to your head to reach for your smart phone. Or respond to that Facebook posting. Or get back to someone on e-mail. I realize that everyone has to earn a living and employers have found a way to tether people to their desk chairs using recharge-able batteries, but forget all that for a minute. No, forget about all that for at least five minutes. Give yourself a positive boost.

Press Start to Continue

I hope you're feeling a surge of confidence as you go forward. Remember that you're "in charge"—in com-mand of the technology and its changes. We all have people in our lives who have, unfortunately, drifted away from our sphere of day-to-day activities. Use the power of your gravity to pull them back with-out any disruption in the space-time continuum. In other words, put the gadgets aside in lieu of some hugs, and see what transpires.

Step 4

Re: Vitalize

10

Your Organic Blueprint

Days 19–23

*"The real danger is not that computers
will begin to think like men, but that men
will begin to think like computers."*

—**Sydney J. Harris**

Get ready to lay out your new approach to technology. It will enforce awareness and establish boundaries for dealing with technology, everything from when to answer the cell phone to when to check e-mail to what necessitates a text message versus a Skype call. It will

Exercise Day 19

Nothing replaces a phone call. Well, okay, a face-to-face encounter is the best (glad you've been paying attention). But when it comes to the power in your devices and services, using them for a conversation is ideal. I know it sounds old-fashioned, but try using a landline for a weekly intimate call to someone you love. Don't go cell to cell or use Skype or Google Voice. Try to arrange a phone call without dropped signals or intrusions (such as a text coming in while on your cell). There is something inherently meaningful

affect your daily schedule and how you interact with your loved ones. The success of this process comes down to you—make balance a priority, and the rewards will manifest. At this point in the diet you're welcome to use your devices whenever you choose—so long as you don't forget your mantra of "how" and "why."

about a landline phone call, and something that's been lost over time thanks to the delay that seems to be a regular (and unwelcome) part of every cell-phone call. So give it a try—use the phone at work if you have to, and rediscover the melodious sounds of a real phone call with a voice you haven't truly heard in a while. Try to use only a landline at home, and keep the cell phone for when you're on the go. I know it's hard—an increasing number of people are abandoning the landline altogether—but see if it still has a place in your home.

Happy E-days Ahead

The alarm clock on our phone goes off, we reach for it or a laptop, and so our e-day begins. We're "on" until we drift off to sleep again sixteen hours later, our devices humming away in their chargers next to the bed. Now that you have freer rein over your technology use again, limiting your e-day is something you and your family have to work on every day. For starters, ensure that your device is not plugged in within arm's reach of your bed. That distance will provide some automatic separation between your place of rest and your greedy gadget. Instead I want you to open your first e-mail of the day while taking your first sip of coffee/tea/soy chai latte—not only will it give you a little time to welcome the morning without a virtual intrusion, but it will also make you stronger and more energetic in your response. But what about later in the day, when you're winding down? It can be hard to determine when it's best to stop responding to e-mails or texts or returning calls.

Take Action: Find a reasonable time of day that marks the end of your e-day, a point in time that means no electronics unless it's an emergency. I encourage you to try to end your e-day around 7:30 p.m. at the latest and, essentially, give yourself a break. Don't just put the devices down—turn them off. Not only will it give you some peace of mind, but it will also help reinforce those boundaries between you and everyone else via your technology. Those e-mails and texts and voice mails will still be there in the morning. And with a restful sleep and a fresh start you may be better armed to deal with them. (I doubt many of us do our best work past 7:30 p.m. after a long workday anyway.) Naturally, if you have a scheduled Skype call with the grandparents in Sweden, then make that happen. But allow the bulk of your electronic bombardment to slip away. There are no boundaries until we begin to set them.

More Positive

Tomas Sander, a senior engineer at HP and a Princeton professor, has written extensively about the positive-computing movement. In many ways he is its chief architect (though he is quick to credit others for inspiration and ideas). He imagines technology that is about not just productivity but also making you the person you want to be and about nurturing relationships, not avoiding them. Positive computing is about consciously enhancing our well-being and flourishing in our jobs and personal lives with the aid of information technology.

As an example, Sander refers to the "emotion walk" designed by British artist Christian Nold in 2000. Nold gave people a GPS device and galvanic skin response (GSR) sensors to measure emotional arousal. What he found was that people had physiological (and therefore measurable and trackable) responses that correlated with places in their neighborhood. He overlaid that data with information from Google Maps and created a trail showing where people felt good—maybe where they could smell fresh bread or see kids playing soccer or hear the sound of running water. People could retrace these routes anytime and use their smart phone to assist them along a particular path. Sander says that's the essence of "positive computing"—finding a place for computing in your life beyond the day-to-day uses. You'd still send e-mails but you'd view your smart phone as more than just something for work. Your computer could monitor everything from how hard you were tapping the mouse to how long you used e-mail to various meetings in your calendar and perhaps offer you messages of support in times of need.

Privacy is clearly an issue in this notion of letting ourselves be integrated with our machines, but isn't this assimilation happening to a certain degree already? How does it also affect those around us? Stone tells us to trust our minds and our bodies, to pay attention to how we feel. Why aren't all these devices and Web sites making us *feel* better? Is it because the technology is too passive and we need it to be more aligned with us as individuals? I'm not suggesting we'll all have a personal robot within the next few years, but think about how you feel toward your technology and how it makes you feel about your environment. Also consider what your actions do to those around you. Your getting a quick

Exercise Day 20

Find your favorite digital photo and make it your splash screen on your smart phone. Don't choose a file photo or a picture of a rock star; pick something meaningful. Seeing it every time you open your phone will change the way you look at your device. Truth is, it's the modern-day equivalent of carrying photo-booth snapshots in your wallet. If your phone allows, it's also worth trying to add a photo to each specific contact, or at least your family and close friends, to see their smiling faces each time they reach out to you. Some smart-phone software, like HTC Sense, will also bring up a reminder of the person's birthday when the call shows up on the screen, thanks to shared Facebook data—a nice combination of real and virtual.

text message while sitting at the dinner table may trigger a brief feeling of excitement but annoy and disgust everyone else at the table. Positive computing is organic and dynamic. It means not just secluding yourself in your bubble of gadgets but considering the ramifications of where it leads you and touches others. Asking questions of ourselves but also listening to that inner voice is so important. Maybe there's a way to maximize that relationship. It's like my friend and producer Rafael Jimenez says: "Work smarter, not harder."

Touchy Techie

Take Action: When Stone talks about getting more in touch with our senses, she really means it. There's no question that walking with your head down, buried in a device, deprives you of seeing the immediate world around you, in some cases when you're driving or sitting in a park or having dinner. The sights, sounds, and smells (remember smells?) around us turn into white noise as we madly type a response or check the latest baseball scores. I know this sounds right out of the 1960s, but for a couple of days spend five minutes receiving sensory information for every fifteen minutes you spend on technology. In other words, if you're texting with someone for fifteen minutes, then pause for five minutes and look around, inhale the air, make note of the things you hear. A plane overhead. A car honking. An argument. Maybe there's an odor of diesel. Did that tree grow that much in the past month? Over the next couple of days, see if those sights and sounds grow slightly more vibrant. Look into people's eyes. The world may open up around you in ways that you'd forgotten. It's a basic trade-off—fifteen for five. It can be indoors or outdoors.

You don't need to get meditative and try to pick up on the vibrations of the universe or something. Just let your primal senses get some time at the forefront of your life. Here's another one: when was the last time you looked up? Our gadgets force us to spend most of our time looking down. It's a wonder that chiropractors haven't had a surge in patients with sore necks. Actually, they probably have (along with sore shoulders and backs from time spent at computer desks). Again, I know it sounds a bit flaky, but go with it. Clouds. The sky. The tops of buildings. What a person is wearing. Observe your environment with an appreciation for what's there. That you're there, too. Plant your feet. Look

Exercise Day 21

Acknowledge your devices in a social setting. These days everyone just throws their phones on the table at a restaurant or bar. They sit there like a silent but deafening distraction just waiting to happen. We can all agree that phones are off limits during meals unless absolutely necessary, but if you are expecting a call at a certain time, make a point of mentioning your device and why you need it readily available. You may find some common ground with the other person about their struggle with technology. See where the act and the discussion lead. It will at least force you to brush up on your conversation skills.

around. It doesn't cost anything, but the rewards can be huge.

You've Got "Tech-sonality"

There was one friend at CBS News who always surprised me with the difference between the way he'd greet me in the hall and his tone in e-mail exchanges. In person, he'd give nothing more than a gruff "hey" or nod or wry smile. That was it. But on e-mail he was engaging, interested, and downright enthusiastic. More than a few of his e-mails even contained exclamation points. What was going on here? It's what I call our "tech-sonality"—how we deal with people online as opposed to offline. My friend's tech-sonality wasn't lining up with his real-life personality. And it bothered me. Why couldn't he be more consistent? (Quick aside—paranoia over what gets written in corporate e-mail thanks to intense monitoring makes me crazy.)

Are you charming and sweet in e-mails but impatient and snarky in meetings? Or perhaps the reverse? We all have slight differences in tone and vocabulary online and offline. Take a minute to think about why that might be so, to consider your online and offline personas. How can you merge them more closely? Don't let your avatar dictate who you are. Make it the opposite.

And don't forget to maximize your face-to-face time when possible. Many of us can get out of practice. Losing the opportunity to gauge facial expressions and reactions may decrease your empathy and therefore your trust, according to Kevin Rockmann

of George Mason University and Gregory North-
craft, a professor of executive leadership at the
University of Illinois who specializes in workplace
collaboration. In their study, two hundred university students formed teams and had to discuss a
serious issue, either nuclear disarmament or price
fixing. Some were requested to have the discussions
via e-mail, some via video conferencing, and some
face to face. The professors then analyzed how effective the groups' discussions had been. In the end,
the ones using that intimate art of in-person conversation got the most done. Now you know why the
secretary of state still needs to fly around the world
to be effective.

If Then, So What?

While doing my undergraduate degree in writing in
the early 1990s, I decided to try my hand at computer programming. I've had an innate interest in
technology since I was a kid largely thanks to my
father, who is an electronics technician by trade and
put the first soldering iron in my hand with only a
low-grade burn, and definitely consider myself a
geek/nerd in a good way. Plus, my mom instilled

in me a curiosity of both the natural and the electronics worlds (she did buy me my first computer, a Commodore VIC-20). But choosing computer programming was a leap, one that came from my desire to not only play the video games but also create them. How hard could it be? So I signed up for a class in Pascal. Never heard of it? Well, for good reason. It's a dense, clumsy, and limited computer language that's now mostly obsolete. But the basis of Pascal (as well as other computing languages, like BASIC, C, Fortran, etc.) can be applied to a Digital Diet approach. Even though I got a D+ in the class, the concept that's stayed with me is "if then." The premise is similar to Newton's law about everything having an equal and opposite reaction. For every decision to write a line of programming, there is a consequence. It might be something as simple as making a document appear larger on the screen or as significant as sinking a battleship in a video game. The point is that every action causes a reaction.

In the modern computer age the if-then idea can serve to remind us of the conscious choices in everything. Nothing we consume in a digital fashion is structured by accident. Everything is designed to create a reaction, from the way ads pop up in your Google searches to the way you get reminded when you're over your limit of text messages. The more you're aware of the if-then rule, the more power you can exert over your own online life. Be aware if, in three clicks, you end up on a site asking for your e-mail address. Don't let down your guard.

The if-then rule also applies to your real-life relations with regard to technology. If you keep checking your BlackBerry while your husband is talking to you, then he might decide to not share his stories in the future. If your children don't balance online time with outside time, then they might become sedentary. If you don't find the time to put down the

Exercise Day 22

Organize a game night with family or friends. In this case, I mean an actual board game. It could be Scrabble or Risk or Boggle, or whatever gets everyone excited. But find a time when you can all sit together, face to face, breathing the same air. Sure, it could be hard to get the kids into it in the beginning, but I find that many times the reluctance turns into "Can't we just play one more round?" after a couple of hours.

gadgets and log out once in a while, then you might lose the ability to appreciate the finer moments in life. Not every "if then" leads to a negative outcome, but it's increasingly important for us to be conscious of the multiple connections and consequences tied to our decisions.

Your Ohm's Law

My father is an electronics technician by trade, and he was always building or fixing something: an LED alarm clock made from a cookie tin, a police-band scanner, a floor lamp crafted from driftwood. I didn't inherit his math skills or the ability to construct an electronics formula. But I loved melting small pieces of solder and watching it drip onto various wires. And I was always fascinated with circuit boards. The intricate design, the minute precision, and the eventual outcome of a tiny bulb lighting up. Just for a minute, imagine that you are the circuit board. Those wires are your blood vessels and those diodes are your organs. (Stay with me here.) The voltage (like a force or energy) is your gadgets and Web sites and all the electronics you use every day. It channels into you like a river. The outcome is the

Exercise Day 23

Try taking a task offline. For example, if you were going to order groceries online, then make a trek to the grocery store. Instead of just ordering a new shirt on the Web, make a trip to your favorite clothier. It'll take more time, but it'll also give you a chance to relax, get a little exercise, and maybe chat with some of the locals.

current or the rate at which that force is flowing. It's easy to get carried away.

The comparison between you and a circuit board is actually not that far-fetched—the truth is that we're composed more of transistors these days than of neurons. Instead of a transistor radio with a handful of transistors, we've now got a Kindle with sixteen billion of them. The average brain is made up of about one hundred billion neurons. The typical consumer owns about twenty-five electronics products; multiply that by sixteen billion transistors per device. Well, you can see how neurons compare. We live in a time of transition, surrounded by transistors. What's missing? The resistors. They are the third element in the relationship between voltage and current. Without the resistors, electrical current would overwhelm a circuit and run rampant. Get to know your own resistors, for you are in control of them. They are the gateways through which you allow technology into your life.

Removing the voltage (i.e., disconnecting from all your devices and Web sites) is certainly one way to eliminate the need for resistance. But most of us need that voltage, that force, in our lives in order to survive and thrive in the twenty-first century. We can, however, harness the power of resistance and funnel that voltage in an effective manner. The tips, tricks, and exercises in this book are meant to serve as your resistors. That might mean only logging into Facebook twice a day for fifteen minutes at a time, or it might mean limiting your texts to twenty-five per day. You have the power to resist when necessary.

Don't Overdo the To-Do List

Rather than start each day with an impossible series of tasks and projects, start with the immediate issues and see what you have time for. Making a giant list of all the things you need to accomplish on a particular day can paralyze you and sap your productivity. If you keep your expectations in check, you might surprise yourself later in the day when you still have energy upon returning home.

Speaking of preparation, make it a rule of thumb to search for directions or confirm a meeting before you get behind the wheel or head out the door. As the father of an infant, my role is often to plot our errands. For example, if we're heading to the pediatrician's office later in the day, I might book a Zipcar, plot the directions and find the best route through Google Maps, and print off a coupon for a nearby parking garage. Yes, each action uses technology, and it's a wonderful thing. The point is to do it in an efficient manner in *advance*. In my case, that means my wife won't be scolding me for texting while driving or getting lost while the baby cries or not finding a parking spot. I can enjoy the experience along the way and be present in the moment.

Take Action: One of the best sites to help you go from the online world to the offline one is Meetup.com. There are more than 2,000 groups who organize a face-to-face "Meetup" through the site. Activities range from belly dancing to hiking to learning to speak Italian. It's all based on where you live, so you can find something nearby. You can even start your own Meetup and invite others to join. Becoming a part of Meetup is as easy as searching a topic or your zip code. (Of course there's also a Meetup app.)

Hitting the Refresh Button

As you head into the home stretch, give yourself some credit. And ask yourself those questions that we brought up at the beginning of the book: Are colors or smells more vibrant? Do you feel more grounded and confident? What is your biggest concern? What are your intentions versus motivations? How are your relations with loved ones? How would you describe your reliance on technology?

I'm hoping your answers have changed. For the better.

11

Sustainable Intake

Days 24–28

"Technology presumes there's just one right way to do things and there never is."

—Robert M. Pirsig

This chapter is about sending you back to the "real world" with renewed confidence and encouragement. It's your blueprint for living beyond the plan. It's also like the reward phase, where we review the concepts and the reasons for adhering to the plan beyond twenty-eight days. You should also take your Virtual Weight Index and compare it

Exercise Day 24

Get out that notebook again and write down the aspects of the diet that frustrated you and the ones that have benefited you. Keep in mind that you can always make changes to your future relationship with technology, but outline how you're feeling now. It's all valuable information.

with the one you took earlier in the diet. I will offer some conclusions on the process and remind you of how it's not about disconnecting—it's about connecting meaningfully. This is the part where you really get motivated to carry on with the process. Go for it!

Inclusion vs. Exclusion

Buying a particular technology product or signing up for a service means a conscious decision to include it in our lives. We see a way for it to benefit us (cheaper, faster, smaller). But often it steals away more of our attention and time. If you signed up for a MySpace account and later jumped over to Facebook and a bit of foursquare but then decided that LinkedIn was more your speed, what happened to your presence in those other social networks? Putting aside the very real concerns over privacy and companies that take your information for marketing, imagine that you're leaving traces of yourself online. Bread crumbs in the form of pixels. Over time, we've all migrated to the Web site du jour or felt the need to upgrade a smart phone or laptop. We've added more e-mail addresses and don't close down the other ones since maybe we used them to sign up for a service. We've become great at including but awful at excluding. In other words, every time you sign up for something new, ask yourself: Is there also something I can power down or deactivate or unsubscribe to? It's right in line with the if-then consequences. Streamline your digital intake. Do you need two cell phones and four e-mail addresses and twenty mailing lists and three social networks? Why? No, really—why? Force yourself to justify all that technology screeching for your attention.

Read Only

In an age of streaming iTunes songs and downloading Netflix, we've all but forgotten terms like

Exercise Day 25

Take a day and see what happens if you only read your personal e-mails and don't respond to them. That's right. No responses at all. If something's an emergency, pick up the phone and call. Allow the e-mails to wash over you throughout the course of the day. Process the content and the sender. Imagine how the person looked and felt while composing the message. Where were they? Did you receive something from a friend on vacation? Can you sense stress from a co-worker? What prompted them to send you a message? There are subtle clues in every e-mail about the state of mind of the sender. And in this case you are solely the receiver, so use your e-mail antenna to tune those signals. You will find that if you ruminate on the content of the messages it will reveal a great deal more than typing out a hurried response.

"CD-ROM." It sounds quaint, doesn't it? Do you recall what the "ROM" part stands for? Read-only memory. It was meant to draw a distinction with RAM (random-access memory). "RAM" (a term still widely used) meant data that could be randomly accessed while it was powered, whereas ROM is simply data that can be displayed and stored but not changed or altered (at least, not easily). An analogy might be a blackboard being written and erased thousands of times a minute (RAM) versus a wall with acrylic paint on it (ROM). This exercise is called "Read Only" because it will involve the way you interact with your e-mail. When was the last time you only read your e-mail and didn't respond? If you're like I was before my Digital Diet, then probably never. E-mails are like a siren song that won't be ignored. They have a tendency to mock you, those unread or unreturned messages, silently nagging you until they get some attention.

Fight Fire with Firewalls

Take Action: Most smart phones these days come with some kind of "airplane mode" setting (the ability to turn off the wireless signal). Even the idea of "airplane mode" is becoming a bit dated, since these days you can use your smart phone to tap into the Wi-Fi on many planes. But it's a setting that can be used anywhere, anytime. The next time you have lunch with someone, consider flipping your phone to airplane mode. Just for the course of the meal. I suspect your lunch date will be most impressed if you show them what you're up to. Make a point of it, talk about it, and then move on.

Exercise Day 26

This may not happen in a day, but consider it. Over the years I've grappled with a relatively simple concern: should I carry around multiple gadgets to do different things or just one gadget? In terms of the Digital Diet, I'm going to have to say one device. Although I sacrifice something in quality (smart-phone cameras, for example, don't have the sophistication of a real digital camera), I'm able to divide my time within the device in a fairly efficient manner and lighten my load considerably. Too much juggling of gadgets leads to distraction and wasted time. Streamline and simplify.

Keeping Tabs on the Monitors

Software engineers and hardware manufacturers seem determined to feed our desire to multitask. They love to include new features or tools, like browser tabs and dual-screen monitors that allow us to do more at one time. These can be dangerous traps that suck away our attention span and generally cause heart palpitations due to information overload. Gone are the days when you might only have one browser window open at a time, working on one task or program. That's so 1995. Today it's about multiple browser windows *and* multiple tabs within those windows. Firefox, Internet Explorer, Chrome—they all offer tabs as a way to easily jump back and forth among various applications. (Tabs allow you to open up multiple Web sites within one browser window.) But think of what this is doing to your brain—it's tabbing it out in the same way. All those tabs demand our attention, and because of the dynamic nature of the Web, each one constantly offers us a new reason to check it (new e-mail arrives, instant message pops up, blog refreshes).

Take Action: I'm not going to suggest that you never use tabs again; that's a bit extreme. Given that so much of what we do is in the "clouds," tabs do allow us to get that information quickly. But consider keeping the tabs within your browser window to a maximum of five. And just one browser window. With five tabs you can clearly read each tab header; you can probably keep up with the information coming in. If you feel like you need some assistance, there's an extension for the Chrome browser called "No More Tabs." It's pretty strict. If you go over five tabs, it will automatically close one of them. (And remember to limit yourself to one active browser window.) The goal is to finish one task at a time. As for dual-screen monitors—well, that's a tough one. I know some people like to use one monitor for something like watching the Dow or NASDAQ and then use the other for their current work. In general I'd have to dissuade you from the use of dual monitors unless you're a graphics or video artist or have two sets of eyeballs. Personally, I find it rather dizzying and quite unnecessary. (The latest trend is dual-touch-screen monitors; one serves as a display and the other as a virtual keyboard/track pad. They may be cool advancements and engineering marvels but are also likely rather unnecessary.) With both tabs and monitors just be conscious of the intrusion in your life. They are options, not requirements. Just like your entire use of technology.

The Scarlet Letter, Twenty-First-Century Style

Now that you've almost completed the Digital Diet, I'm going to ask you to become vigilant in monitoring other people's digital behavior, especially your family's and friends'. One of my experiences with that philosophy involved a flight to San Francisco. At the last minute I was bumped up to first class and excitedly gathered my travel goodies en route to my new seat. Since my wife was five months pregnant at the time, I wanted a last little check-in and a chance to share my upgraded seat status. Then I heard "The boarding doors have closed," which is now synonymous with "Shut off your damn gadgets so we can depart."

So I madly typed a few lines to my wife and waited for her to respond. I used the in-flight magazine to conceal my criminal activity from the flight attendant, but the man next to me had taken notice and said, "What gives, buddy?" I halfheartedly tried to explain the fact that using a cell phone probably

wouldn't make the plane crash, but he wasn't interested. He told me that everyone else had to shut
down their devices, including him, so I should com-
ply, too. After all, we wanted to take off in a timely
manner. I was red-faced and sheepish. The point
is that we're all fallible. I was using my phone for
what I deemed to be a worthy and worthwhile en-
deavor (texting my pregnant wife), but it impinged
on someone around me (several people around me)
and I was selfishly caught up in my own world. This
served as a reminder for me, and I was ultimately
grateful. Sometimes a little slap on the head can
shake loose some real common sense. And even
though I'd previously been the passenger who was
annoyed with the *other* person who wouldn't shut
off their device, I somehow became him.

That scolding stuck with me. That guy had the
gumption to express his opinion, and he snapped
me back into place. I encourage you to do that with
your circle of loved ones, too. If Uncle Gary always
puts his cell phone on the table during Sunday din-
ners, then politely ask him to leave it in his jacket
until everyone has finished dessert. If you're trying
to talk to your husband but he's doing one of those
text-nod-text-*mmmhmm*-text-*mmmhmm*-nod
combos and he's clearly distracted and not listen-

ing, then stop talking. Just stop midsentence. If he's not a total cad, then I guarantee he will stop long enough for you to say, "Honey, I'll finish what I'm saying when you put that down for a minute." It's the modern version of the silent treatment.

It begins with exchanging opinions with people you know and love and trust and not letting rude behavior slide by. Giving them a slightly hard time about it (or their giving you one) helps change the social norms in your relationship. You can't continue to manage your digital intake on your own; you should at least try to project how important digital limitations are to those around you. Make sure your kids are aware of what the house rules are with regard to technology; tell your friends you hope they won't check their e-mail when you're out for coffee. It's time for our society to set some rules for what

Exercise Day 27

Be brave and call someone out on his or her annoying or rude behavior when it comes to using technology in public. Of course, you must expect to receive the same treatment from others if you trip up yourself.

is polite and impolite in terms of gadget use in social situations. Set those rules for yourself, and try to impress them upon others as well, respectfully but forcefully. Be careful, and be smart. But don't be afraid to poke.

The Ongoing Social-Network Battle

In August 2010 Google's CEO, Eric Schmidt, said that young people may one day need to change their names to escape their troubled social-network past. Is that not a frightening thought? Beyond the concern over privacy is the one about identity—while we all grow and change and develop over our adult years, does the Web 2.0 generation need a "clear cache" button to start their mature years? Is it becoming like purging a criminal record before becoming an adult? And what feeds this behavior?

Suffice to say that while social networks like Facebook have become part of the vernacular (and even the subject of feature films), there have been few studies done on the psychological tractor beam that pulls people into them. One was done through York University in Toronto. Soraya Mehdizadeh, a bachelor of science student, interviewed one hundred randomly selected Facebook users from the York campus. These students allowed Mehdizadeh to code their Facebook pages, which meant monitoring their activity and assigning it various scores. For example, Mehdizadeh was most interested in the students' "About Me," main photo, first twenty pictures, status updates, and Notes section. Any changes to these pages (the frequency and content) could be tabulated and compared over time. The key was photos with self-aggrandizing poses (I've been guilty on numerous occasions) or status updates that ventured into self-promotion (also guilty), like "I'm so glamorous I bleed glitter." This information was cross-referenced with content updates, frequency of logging on, and duration of time on the site.

What Mehdizadeh discovered was that both gender and self-esteem played a prominent role. Men displayed more self-promotional information in the "About Me" and Notes sections, while women offered more self-promotional material in the form of the main photo. A previous German study had found that self-esteem did not play a role in social-network activity, but Mehdizadeh concluded that those with low self-esteem were much more involved and sought greater return on the investment in their profiles.

Have I struggled with this? To a certain degree, yes. But given that there are now more than five hundred million users of Facebook alone, we have to wonder (a) how many of us are suffering from low self-esteem without realizing it, (b) what technology is doing to feed our desire for attention and acceptance, and (c) what we can do to find these things beyond our smart phone or computer screen.

But let's move forward with social networks—they aren't going away, and if you choose to stick with them, then embrace the experience in a positive fashion. Sharing photos on social networks can be a great way to disseminate shots of babies or weddings or vacations. But consider keeping out the drunken party ones or the ones that reveal too much about your personal address. And always be considerate when tagging photos (attaching people's names to them). Try logging out of your social network if you're not active on it. Trolling through pages and pages can often trigger feelings of jealousy or frustration. Certainly, if you're interested in what your best friend or your favorite aunt posted, check it out. But also remember to extend that relationship into the real world or outside the social network when possible. Make a phone call. See what the kids are up to outside. Don't exist purely in the social-network environment. You could also omit a status update on occasion. Why does everyone need to know what you're doing or where you are all the time? Make your life experiences more personal and confine them to a smaller sphere (e.g., only the people actually with you at the movie). Finally, don't obsess about your social network. It isn't you. Take the energy and the time you used to spend crafting some cluttered profile page and engage more with your family. Give someone you love a hug. Or two. Life is short. Don't let social-network screen time dictate your real-life social nature and experiences.

And yet we must remind ourselves that social net-

Exercise Day 28

Take an online conversation offline. In other words, if you're instant messaging with someone, take it to a phone call (preferably landline). Or if you're texting, set up a coffee date. Be aware of whom you decide to engage in the physical world—what does that say about them and your relationship? Conversely, what does it say about people you avoid doing it with?

works serve their purpose, too. As you now know, I returned to Facebook and Twitter, albeit in a limited fashion. I stripped away the status updates, minimized my log-ins to two or three times per day for a maximum of five to ten minutes, and sought other forms of communication when it came to connecting with loved ones and real friends. Was I grappling with social networks or self-image? Likely a combination of both. But I know that I'm not alone. And I know that still others find solace in social networks in ways that skip over narcissism and self-indulgence.

One such person is my friend and former journalism school classmate Ian Clayton. Clayton and I were close during our years of graduate studies and both very involved with the development of the school's first foray into online journalism (back then I actually hand-coded the first editions of our monthly newsmagazine, *Thunderbird*). We grew apart over the years, but I knew Clayton was close with his mother, and in 2006 he watched as she met an untimely demise. Yet it was only in 2010 that he confided in me how social networks aided in his recovery from such a deep tragedy. He recounts how he eventually crept into Facebook after giving it much reflection:

Part of the reason for that was that since my mom passed away in 2006 I would have been too depressed to try and create a page like this and be exposed to people's triumphs, jokes, and (sometimes trivial) complaints, etc. (I mean, I didn't even listen to any music etc. for the better part of a year after she died because nothing connected to me, seemed important or relevant and so on).

I think one of the main things that first caused me to create a page was so that I could scan some pictures I had of her and keep them in a place which was (somewhat) safe, i.e., if something happened to the physical copies. And I wanted some kind of way for her to live on, for at least some people (I don't expect most people I am "friends" with have looked at them either) to see how beautiful she was for me—because she was gone. I also—and I know you mentioned this—had this feeling that I needed to put some of my own pictures down, mainly for myself even—almost to remind myself that I had done all these different things, traveled to different places and so on. Because I wasn't really pursuing my earlier plan to be a rock star and be "immortalized" in videos or some dumb thing, it was a place for me to put together some images from my life.

It's an insightful lesson for us all. Indeed, if we're honest with ourselves, part of the motivation for collecting our photos and updates and travels on a virtual map is to remind ourselves that *we were here*. It's more self-affirming than self-promoting. While Facebook and MySpace and Twitter gained increasing popularity over blogs, thanks to the ability to advertise our number of "friends" or "followers" and compete with others to carve out the best e-landscape, many of us might remain members of social networks for no other reason but to preserve our selves in a way that we can see and absorb. It's meaningful to look back at photos from that 2007 Halloween party or that 2008 graduation ceremony or that 2009 birthday party. This is another positive aspect of social networks. That time line of your life can provide some perspective, and there are few opportunities to see all your photos in one place along with descriptions of them. And why not? Again, it's about balance and purpose. Know why you're there. A little reminiscing is fine. But don't be afraid to delete old stuff. Every so often when you log on to a social network, remind yourself of the reason and the rationale.

The Business of Networking

It comes as no surprise that social networks, smart phones, texting, etc., can be invaluable tools when it comes to a prosperous business existence. But it's not just because they're ways of direct communication. It's also because they provide a social lubrication that can aid any business encounter. I'm constantly reminded of this through my presence on LinkedIn. I find it useful, and many of my peers do, too. Many prospective employers will dive into social networks like LinkedIn (and search engines) to do some homework. If you're in the market for a job and you have no presence at all (or if it's outdated), that can be alarming or confusing for an employer. Sometimes making a connection over a shared hobby or favorite destination can open doors. Reaching out via a short message within a shared social network is fine if it's aimed at the business audience (as LinkedIn is). But it's best to keep contacts with prospective job interviewers off sites like Facebook or MySpace, since they're deemed more social. That would just be an unusual way to start a business relationship (unless perhaps you're already friends with the person). In my opinion, it's ideal to take any business encounter off social networks and into e-mail or a phone call or a face-to-face meeting as soon as possible. But having a social-network footprint can certainly be beneficial as a starting point. Naturally, there is the potential for abuse as one side or the other boasts or downright lies about their accomplishments or qualifications, but ulti-

Exercise: Future

You've made it! Your exercise today is to simply take a deep breath. It's now time to incorporate technology in ways that please and satisfy you to the best of your ability. You've persevered through some obstacles and hopefully found ways to maximize technology in your life. There will be good days and bad days. Easy ones and hard ones. No one is perfect at accepting and dealing with technology—we all struggle with it at times, me included. But arm yourself and feel confident that you've sought a heightened awareness.

mately it often proves to be a useful gateway to real social interaction.

The bottom line is that incorporating social networks into your life can be done for the right reasons and with optimum results. Collecting photos and reflections can be about self-affirmation rather than self-aggrandizement. And befriending business associates is clearly a solid way to leverage social networks and make them work for you (while you seek work). As for the advantages in the dating world—well, that's a whole other book.

We'll Be Right Back After These Messages

Moving forward, your greatest project will be to manage your online communications, such as e-mail, texts, instant messages, Skype chats, Meebo exchanges, Gmail chat, and every other way that you convey your work directives or friendly banter or love notes. Here's the easiest approach: remember the filters. Go on, be a filter ninja. Set up one filter that sifts your primary contacts (boss, loved ones, sensei) into one folder. Create another that filters e-mails sent directly to you (i.e., with your name in the "To" box). Filters aren't perfect, and it will require some work to set them up, but it might diffuse the constant e-mail attack happening in your in-box. Although e-mail just ain't cool for the kids anymore (they've moved on), the reality is that it isn't going away as a tool for business and staying in touch anytime soon. So make the best of it. Be decisive, be active, and don't look back.

The same goes for texts—I know many carriers offer unlimited programs, but aim for a more limited stance. You don't have to max out your phone's ability to keep sending texts. Think before you send. Consider the quality, the content, and the motivation behind each message. Are you missing something in real life (like that truck barreling down on you) while you're busy texting, "no way that 'Bucks muffin ws 300 calories more lik 3000"? You get my point. With instant messages—well, aim to be considerate. Don't just insert yourself into someone's routine. Ask if it's a good time, see if they're busy, and then get to the point (if it's business) or perhaps take it to the phone or in person if it's more intimate. Look, I can't read your e-mails and tell you what to write, but I know the importance of e-mails and texts and instant messages. Recall that my wife and I courted (in 2001) through e-mails and instant messages, and at one point in our relationship she printed all of them out and pasted them into a scrapbook. It was actually one of the best presents I've ever received, and it reminded me of the power of the written word in any form. But infuse your communication with your mind and your heart, and it will pay dividends. Don't waste your time online with anything less.

You, in the Future

Socrates famously encouraged followers, "Know thyself." Today, it's often more about "show thyself." We're so eager and desperate to keep up and reinvent our online images and stay ahead of the information avalanche that we rarely turn the spotlight on ourselves and internalize our thoughts. That's where technology stops making us better and starts separating us from our true selves. Don't be that person. And don't let it happen to those around you. You may have read through this entire book and feel too intimidated to enact the entire diet. That's fine. It's meant to work in pieces and stages and phases. Or you might wish to extrapolate some of the diet and apply it to your colleague or your children or your spouse. My wife and I do it to each other all the time. We challenge each other and question our consumption and try to keep it in balance. Just work, a little, every day, and you'll be surprised how far you can go. Sticking to it is not easy—but neither is exercise or regular dieting. I fall off the Digital Diet bandwagon from time to time, and you will, too. But no matter what, you can always work to be more aware of your digital intake. Challenge the role of these sites and devices in your life and force them to earn their place.

I'm reminded of the Latin motto from my high school in Victoria, British Columbia: *"nulla praemia sine opera."* Loosely translated that means, "no reward without effort." It's stuck with me my whole life, and I've tried to infuse that concept throughout the Digital Diet. I suppose the exercise equivalent would be "no pain, no gain." None of this is going away. The only way technology gets truly removed from our lives is if there's a solar storm on par with the one in the movie *2012.* Unlikely.

We aren't analog creatures anymore. We won't be reverting to living in huts and cooking over fires and logging in to CompuServe anytime soon. All of our online communication isn't moving offline anytime soon either. Our collective inertia carries us forward, and I, for one, am excited about what it will bring. But remember to think about what matters and what you *feel*. Analyze. Be aware. Don't be a tech patsy. Interact and be inter*active*. You know what works for your family and your life and your job. It's not like there aren't choices—you just need to make the right ones.

One of the last thoughts I'll leave you with is from one of my personal icons and idols: SpongeBob SquarePants. As we all know, SpongeBob is a sponge. Not just any sponge, of course, a sponge that has an infectious laugh and an insatiable curiosity. But SpongeBob knows when he's had enough. He knows when to try something new. He doesn't let Patrick or Gary or Squidward force him into doing anything. He makes up his own mind and lets the chips fall where they may. And when it comes to technology, it's okay to be a sponge. Soak it up. Try it out. But remember to wring the excess out of your life periodically. Maintain an optimistic outlook—it's your Digital Diet!

Take Action: There's no absolute or perfect scenario with the Digital Diet. Just as every food diet has variations and debates and detractors, so, too, does the digital one. The point is to experiment.

Perhaps at this stage of your life certain components of this program will work better than others. And maybe some won't fit your situation. But before you make excuses about why you can't try to trim a habit or change your actions, give yourself permission to see what works. Experiment. Mix and match.

A Life Choice

On a final note, late in 2010 I got the chance to interview Phyllis Greene, who had friended me on Facebook a couple of years earlier. That may not strike you as out of the ordinary until you learn that Phyllis was ninety years old at the time. You read that right. Phyllis was active on Facebook nearly from the beginning of its popularity, and she maintained a regular blog, too. When she first friended me, I thought for sure it had to be a prank. But she was the real thing. Actually, as Bono would put it, even better than the real thing. You see, when I met Phyllis she was confined to her bed, accompanied by her daughter D. G. Fulford, and living out the remaining months or weeks or hours of her life in hospice care. Her heart was giving out, but her mind sure wasn't. She was as vibrant as I'd imagined she would be given the energy and life of her postings online. When I visited her, she told me that she would keep blogging until the end.

What does this have to do with the Digital Diet? Well, it's all about perspective. Phyllis has kept a dedicated online presence over the last several years and is fearless in her pursuit of understanding computers and the Web, but she can put away the laptop and focus on the person in the room without missing a beat. Over the last dozen or so years, she took the time to rekindle her relationship with her daughter, D.G., and the two of them wrote a book about it together called *Designated Daughter: The Bonus Years With Mom*. Phyllis found a way to be at peace with her family, fulfill her own life after the passing of her beloved husband, and embrace technology in a way that opened her musings from her bedroom in Columbus, Ohio, to the rest of the world. She wrote about her thoughts on hospice, about her relationship with D.G., and about her family. She also jotted down some thoughts about her time on the planet that she thought the grandkids might like to read one day (her granddaughter often posts on Phyllis's Facebook wall—how many grandparents can say that?). I feel that if Phyllis, near the end of her life, can find a way to successfully integrate technology and keep perspective on her existence, then she's a true role model. Indeed, her vivacity and desire to "carpe diem" while maintaining a healthy Digital Diet may be a universal lesson—for the history books. To me, Phyllis embodies the pinnacle of "positive computing."

It's never too late or too early to embark on the Digital Diet.

Ten Digital Diet Rules to Live By

1. *Avoid tech turds.* Don't just dump your smart phone on the table at a restaurant or at home. Keep it in your pocket or purse unless it's critical to have it out. If you must have it out, acknowledge its presence and inform your companions that you'll check it only in an emergency. It's a courtesy that you'd appreciate, too.

2. *Live your life in the real world.* If you must post a status update or tweet or blog about

something in your life, then make sure it's
something you'd be willing to announce to
anyone you know face to face.

3. *Ask yourself whether you really need that
gadget.* There are tons of cool stuff in the tech
world, and some of it might even improve your
or your family's life, but don't feel compelled to
buy every new toy that comes out. Before you
make a digital purchase, question its necessity.

4. *Seek tech support.* Navigating the wilds of
the wired world can sometimes be too much
to handle alone. It's okay to ask for help,
and it's also okay to use technology to help
"outsource self-control" when needed. Check
out the many programs that can assist with
budgeting your time online.

5. *Detox regularly.* Once you've completed the
Digital Diet, return to the detox phase one
day a month. You can do this as a family, too.
Use that day as a touchstone to remember
what life can be like without technology.

6. *Sleep device-free.* Move your chargers out of
the bedroom to another room in the house,
and let your devices live there overnight.
They need a break from you, too.

7. *It's either the human or the device.* Work toward choosing people over the device. Yes, there'll be times when it's tricky or nearly impossible to choose between your smart phone or laptop and paying attention to your child or your loved one or your friend, but try to use your devices more on your own time rather than during the time you share with others.

8. *Remember the "if/then" principle.* Choices that you make in the virtual world can have an impact in the real one. For example, if you don't find the time to put down the gadgets and log out once in a while, then you might lose the ability to appreciate the finer moments in life.

9. *Structure your e-day.* Work toward a finite beginning and end to your connectedness. In other words, dive into the gadgets and the e-mail and the texts only when you've composed yourself in the morning. When you're ready to unplug in the evening, do it without reservation and focus on what—and who—is immediately around you.

10. *Trust your instincts.* If you think you might be spending too much time being a voyeur on

social networks or playing online games or endlessly texting, then you probably are. That little voice knows when it's all become too much. Listen to it. Pursue the ultimate goal of balance and awareness.

Epilogue: Testimony

Here, in Teisha Stalling's own words, is how she felt after following her twenty-eight-day Digital Diet plan following our appearance on *The Dr. Oz Show*:

This journey was a difficult but rewarding one. When I first accepted the challenge I wasn't completely sure that I was going to follow through with it. I was reluctant at the least to detox for 28 days. I wasn't sure that life without being always "connected" was possible. Since I was a child, I liked to keep up with the latest and greatest gadgets and devices.

Nonetheless I took on the challenge and to my surprise it was extremely fulfilling. I got to see how much of an actual life I was missing out on. I was communicating in person with people again as I did before technology. I never realized how impersonal my communication had become until this detox. I was interacting with my laptop and my phone more than I was interacting with my friends and family.

Upon first learning of the detox plan I just knew that this was a plan for disaster. "There is no way humanly possible that I can go from a full-fledged addiction to technology to just checking e-mails once a day!" was the one thought that was running through my mind.

Then to add insult to injury, the plan included exercise. Now granted I did gain a little weight, but was there really a connection between my technology use and my weight gain?

Even after all of these reservations I decided to take a full plunge into the plan. During the 28 days I didn't have any major detox issues as I thought I would. The first week actually flew by without any serious detox issues. Checking my e-mail once a day actually wasn't so bad. I did miss my texting and my instant messaging a lot but I was able to manage. The second, third and fourth week, things just got so much easier.

The question in my mind by the end of the plan was no longer "How can I live without technology?" but rather "Why did I need so much technology again?"

I have lost about 15 pounds since I have started the technology detox plan and I am continuing to lose weight. The eight hours that I used to spend sitting in front of my laptop, iPod, or phone has been replaced with walking or simple exercise routines at home.

I have also noticed a change in my overall health. I have suffered from migraines since I was a child and on average I would experience 4–5 headaches a week. After lightening my technology load, the frequency and severity of the headaches has decreased.

I also have noticed a significant decrease in crampy fingers, lower back pain and neck pain. My sleep patterns have improved and I always seem to awake with that "well rested" feeling. I did however realize that I was trying to suppress different emotions that I didn't want to deal with by overdosing on technology. I was able to get those things on track after the detox plan revealed it to me.

This plan was so manageable that it took me from being a technology addict to a technology user. I regained actual connections with people. I am so grateful that I had the opportunity to try this technology detox plan because life is a lot less stressful when you are not worried about always checking texts, e-mails or social-networking messages. The plan helped me to realize that technology is a good thing as long as it is used in moderation. I do not see myself going back to the tech addict life ever again.

And Finally, a Welcome "By-product"

During the course of this book, I've referenced that my wife and I were pregnant and that we've now become new parents. Well, I firmly believe that it never would've happened without a better approach to my technology consumption. Granted, my last job required that I travel a lot, and it does turn out that being in the same zip code markedly aids the insemination process. (Who knew?) But I also learned to be more in the moment when I was physically present.

I feel as though my own rebirth ultimately made possible the birth of our daughter, Kylie. My improved relationships with my wife and family gave me a new perspective on my future. Of course, now I have baby gadgets on the brain (video monitors, mattress sensors, breast pumps)—but I'm determined to keep a smart phone out of her hand at least until she's past the teething stage. I can only hope this book will open the same doors for you, in both your mind and your day-to-day dealings.

There is no one-size-fits-all route for finding our way through the labyrinth of twenty-first-century life. If nothing else, know that you can do it. Face the challenges head on. It's worth it. And it won't take long to see some of the benefits, for both you and your family.

I'm here with you, grappling and navigating and, sometimes, failing. It's okay to get frustrated and annoyed. It's okay to look at others in your circle and curse them for their apparent control of the modern reality. You'll get there. We all will. Zero in on what matters, and no one knows that better than you do.

Sure, your job and your family and your friends will put demands on you and this Digital Diet program won't always work. It's about hanging on to the essentials, the core. And seek support from those around you.

As you struggle with your Digital Diet, please feel free to message me or ask for advice (daniel .sieberg@gmail.com). I mean it. I may not be able to get back to you immediately (especially when adhering to my own Digital Diet plan), but I'm here. When I used to coach youth soccer in Canada, I would often be shouting the loudest words of encouragement from the sidelines—imagine that I'm doing that with you now. The solution to technology overload is quite literally in the palm of your hand.

With Gratitude

To my beautiful and elegant wife, Shanon Cook, whose selfless guidance, boundless love, and unvarnished input (in no particular order) have helped me be a better man and writer. To my daughter, Kylie, who inspired me during the writing process with kicks and cartwheels in the womb. To my parents, Geraldine Laundy and Douglas Sieberg, who, despite going their separate ways when I was seven years old, kept me on the straight and narrow and somehow managed to be the best parents who didn't live together. To my sister Jennifer Sieberg (RN), who still battles her brain tumor but doesn't let it define her and who is also profoundly optimistic in a way that only a clever and seasoned soul can be. To James and Faye Cook, whose support and encouragement means more to me than they know. To my steadfast and talented editor, Mary Choteborsky of Crown, without whose vision this project would not have been possible. To my tireless literary agent at CAA, Simon Green, and his delightful assistant, Caitlin Hoyt, and to my TV agent at CAA, Andrea

Ross, who has never doubted me despite my many stages of neurosis. To producer Allison Markowitz at *The Dr. Oz Show*, who helped initially structure the Digital Diet idea and injected it with her contagious enthusiasm. To my writing professors throughout high school and university, but mostly to Mr. Lampard at Mt. Douglas Senior High for encouraging me to turn inward when the words on the page weren't turning out. To my valued colleagues from ABC News, BBC News, CBS News, PBS, CNN, MSNBC, *Details* magazine, the *Vancouver Sun*, and elsewhere who have kept me on track, called my bluff, and steered me in the right direction when I fell off course. To my first newspaper/magazine boss, who paid me four cents per word. To my dear friends and loved ones around the world who kept me motivated (you know who you are). To my assistant, David Miller, who provided valuable research. And to the first person who introduced me to the inter-webs—I've forgotten your name, but I'll always remember the result.

About the Author

Daniel Sieberg is the host of *Tech This Out!* on ABC News NOW and contributes science and technology stories to other ABC News broadcasts including *Nightline* and *Good Morning America*. He is also a featured contributor at *Details* magazine, BBC World News America, PBS, MSNBC, CBS Sunday Morning, the Discovery Channel, and a variety of other networks. He was the CBS News science and technology correspondent from December 2006 to February 2010, reporting for the *CBS Evening News with Katie Couric*, *The Early Show*, *CBS Sunday Morning*, CBS Radio, and CBSNews.com. From 2000 to 2006 Sieberg was the technology correspondent for CNN, CNN International, and HLN. He also hosted *Next@CNN*, a weekly broadcast about science, technology, space, and environment.

Sieberg has been nominated for four News & Documentary Emmy Awards and won accolades from the likes of the Society of Environmental Journalism and the World Technology Network. In 2007, he was named a *Portfolio* magazine "Business Broadcasting All-Star," and he is a recipient of Canada's Rafe Mair Award for public-service journalism.

His written work has appeared in the *Huffington Post*, *Details*, Oprah.com, Salon.com, *Time*, and many other publications. He has served as an analyst for PBS's *Frontline*, NPR, BBC Radio, Fuse.tv, CourtTV, and Animal Planet. Between 1998 and 2000 Sieberg was a daily reporter for the *Vancouver Sun*, covering technology, business, and civic issues.

Sieberg has a bachelor's degree in writing from the University of Victoria and a master's degree in journalism, specializing in technology, from the University of British Columbia. He lives in New York City with his delightful wife, precious daughter, and irascible beagle. This is his first book.